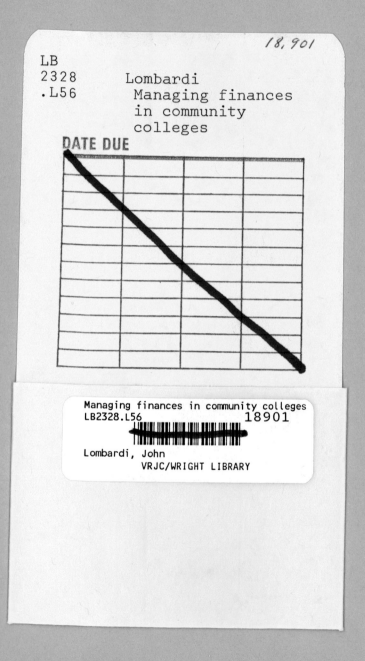

John Lombardi

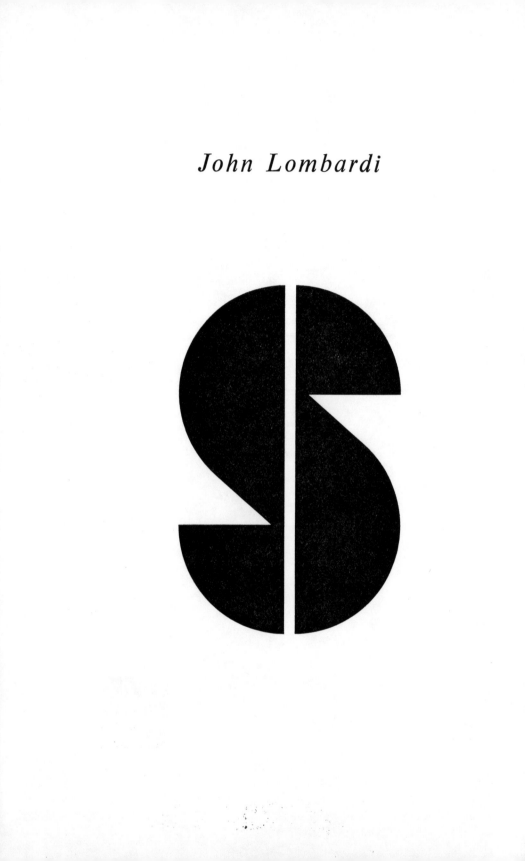

MANAGING
FINANCES
IN
COMMUNITY
COLLEGES

Jossey-Bass Publishers

San Francisco • Washington • London • 1973

MANAGING FINANCES IN COMMUNITY COLLEGES
by John Lombardi

Copyright © 1973 by: Jossey-Bass, Inc., Publishers
615 Montgomery Street
San Francisco, California 94111

&

Jossey-Bass Limited
3 Henrietta Street
London WC2E 8LU

Library of Congress Catalogue Card Number LC 73-10939

International Standard Book Number ISBN 0-87589-199-3

Manufactured in the United States of America

JACKET DESIGN BY WILLI BAUM

FIRST EDITION

Code 7340

The Jossey-Bass Series
in Higher Education

❀❀❀❀❀❀❀❀❀❀❀❀❀❀❀❀❀❀❀❀❀❀❀❀❀❀

Portions of this work were provided by

ERIC
Clearinghouse for Junior Colleges
University of California, Los Angeles

ARTHUR M. COHEN, *director*

*The ERIC (Educational Resources Information Center)
program is sponsored by the
United States Department of Health, Education, and Welfare,
National Institute of Education.
The points of view expressed here do not necessarily represent
official National Institute of Education position or policy.*

Preface

Until a decade ago financing the public educational system seemed to be one of the most secure political activities. Education ranked with church and home as one of the bulwarks of society. During the last ten years, however, public education has lost much of its hold. Though educational institutions still attract millions of youngsters each September, public education is in the midst of a financial crisis. In the first part of *Managing Finances in Community Colleges,* I explore how this change has come about as it relates to the particular concern of the book—the public community college (also called junior colleges, two-year colleges, or city colleges).

In the second part of the book, attention focuses on the sources of revenue, including observations on the future prospects for an increase in revenue from each of five sources. How educators are adjusting to the financial crisis is the theme of the third part. In essence the second and more particularly the third parts contain suggestions and examples of strategies and practices that are helping educators adjust to the crisis.

Because the crisis touches all segments of education, at times the discussion relates to the total educational community. These references cannot be avoided since all public institutions derive their funds from the same sources. Whether educators desire it or not, they are competitors among themselves and with other public institutions for financial support. As far as possible, I exclude here the branches of four-year colleges and universities that, though two years in length, are integral parts of the parent institutions and, consequently, not independent.

Comparisons among colleges and other institutions are made here for purposes of perspective only. They must be interpreted with caution because the data on which they are based are often not truly comparable. Comparisons with four-year colleges, universities, and secondary schools, when necessary, are made with even more reservations and never to enhance the position of the community colleges at the expense of the other institutions. If the community colleges cannot prove their worth to the students and the community, invidious comparisons will not help them.

Managing Finances in Community Colleges is based on my experience as a community college instructor and administrator and as an accrediting commission examiner; on information gathered from ERIC files, college and state reports, visits to many colleges, questionnaires, consultations with community college educators and scholars; and on wide reading of professional journals, newspapers, periodicals, and books.

Objectivity toward a dynamic institution is not easy to come by. Each person looks at the institution from a particular vantage point; he is understandably influenced by many diverse factors. As Toynbee wrote, objectivity in a pure form is impossible even if one is treating long-forgotten civilizations. Each author brings to his work all the prejudices acquired over his lifetime. Even as he selects the various topics and the facts concerning them, an author is influenced by his biases. The most that one can hope to accomplish is to report and interpret the "facts" as honestly as possible.

In one way or another I have expressed appreciation to the many individuals who supplied me with the information used in the preparation of *Managing Finances in Community Colleges*. Particularly gratifying, as well as helpful, was the graciousness with which my requests for information or materials were answered.

At home in the ERIC office I imposed on every member of the staff for service. Arthur M. Cohen, director, and Florence B. Brawer, coordinator of special projects, supported and encouraged me to continue. I am indebted to Beverly A. Harris for editing and keeping the manuscript within bounds, to Kary A. Mercer for typing and retyping various revisions, and to Marcia Boyer for keeping track of the manuscript as it passed from hand to hand during its preparation. Young Park, president of North Peralta College (Oakland, California), formerly of the ERIC staff, assisted me in gathering information on state and college finances.

Los Angeles
September 1973

JOHN LOMBARDI

Contents

THREE: CORRECTING FINANCIAL IMBALANCE

MANAGING FINANCES
IN COMMUNITY COLLEGES

Chapter I

❀❀❀❀❀❀❀❀❀❀❀❀❀❀❀❀❀❀❀❀❀❀❀❀❀❀❀

External Factors

Although the financial crisis in education began some time ago, it reached serious proportions only in the 1960s. Until the 1960s, community colleges were treated generously. During the first fifteen years after World War II they made advances in numbers of students and colleges and the establishment of community colleges in more than 80 percent of the states. In the 1960s universal higher education through the sophomore year seemed an achievable goal. An outcome of the tremendous growth was the initially favorable attention community colleges attracted—attention which became more questioning as expansion absorbed an increasingly large proportion of public funds.

1

As a consequence of this change in public attitudes, educators are now encountering resistance to their requests for funds necessary to meet the needs of increasing numbers of students enrolling in the colleges. The most notable evidence of this shift from the highly favorable climate of the 1950s and early 1960s is the voters' presently negative response to requests for increased taxes and bond issues for capital outlay. The downward trend of voter approval became apparent during 1967, when half the bond issues failed to gain approval in California, Florida, Kansas, Michigan, New Hampshire, and New Jersey. Nationwide, voters defeated educational bond issues in more than 34 percent of these referendums (*School Management*, 1968, p. 34). The next year proved to be even more dismal; at least 40 percent of all bond issues failed. In 1969 voters rejected 43 percent of the education issues (*U.S. News and World Report*, 1969, p. 36).

Sensing hostile public reaction, educators and trustees have become reluctant to submit tax proposals and bond issues to the electorate—with good reason. Even the few measures presented to the voters in 1970 made a poor showing. The continuing public indifference toward education was demonstrated by the defeat of ten statewide referendums; half the tax-hike proposals in Illinois; and similar measures in Alabama, Arkansas, and California. The experience of the Junior College District of St. Louis in four tax elections since the district was formed in 1962 offers another illustration of the taxpayers' disenchantment. Successively the percentage of affirmative votes went down from 75 to 60 to 46 to 45. This unfavorable attitude toward bond issues continues throughout the nation.

At the same time, by approving water pollution and clean air projects, voters leave little doubt about their disaffection for education. Education has ceased to have number one priority. Not all educators deceived themselves on the voters' attitude. Some realized early that the mystique of education was shattered when the promised millennium failed to materialize.

The stress on accountability is partially the result of the questioning attitude of many citizens who believe that the schools are not accomplishing what they claim. This skepticism has been most severe at the elementary level, where schools seem unable to improve reading and arithmetic instruction. Community colleges are criticized for the lack of formal evaluation of courses or programs, inadequacy of placement and counseling services for occupational students, dearth of descriptive data about the developmental remedial mission, and the high dropout rate among transfer students (Chadwin, 1973). Also disillusioning has been the high unemployment rate among college graduates, especially teaching majors and those released from industries associated with air transportation and space exploration. A public opinion poll in late 1972 reported that only 33 percent of the public had "a great deal of confidence in educators," compared with 37 percent in 1971 and 61 percent in 1966 (*Chronicle of Higher Education,* Dec. 4, 1972, pp. 1–2).

These alleged shortcomings and the unemployment situation are undermining the belief that the more education a person has the larger his earning power will be. At the same time, wages for workers in many industries such as truck driving, air conditioning, and building trades are approaching the salaries of many college-educated people. Some are claiming that a college education is not a must for success in modern society.

A Supreme Court decision of June 7, 1971, which upheld laws requiring a two-thirds vote for approval of bond issues, gave school and college educators a severe jolt. Many of them were looking forward to a decision consonant with the one-man, one-vote rule of the Warren Court. If a simple majority were the rule, 90 percent of all California bond issues from January 1 to June 7, 1971, would have passed (*Los Angeles Times,* 1971f).

Most of the examples cited are locally controlled colleges, supported in large part by property taxes, which must submit their requests to the taxpayers. The plight of the state-supported colleges is no less severe. The Kentucky colleges, which suffer from inadequate support for continuing education and community service programs (Hartford, 1971, pp. 35–36), have had as difficult a financial time as any in the country.

Many factors account for this turnabout from high public favor to disaffection; from relatively high financial stability to near insolvency. Some are traceable to the commissions and omissions of educators; others to changing standards and mores of society—such as the movement to deemphasize the tradition of going to college as the main outlet for high school graduates. The turnabout affects most segments of public and private education. Arguments that a public that spends such large sums on automobiles, space explorations, and sport spectacles can and should expend more on education have little effect. The public, given the choice, may choose—some say is choosing—them over education.

One possible cause of public disaffection might be student activism. Community colleges (to a lesser extent perhaps than the universities) suffered from the disturbances of the 1960s. To the public at large, colleges seem to have become places where students are taught to undermine the virtues that have traditionally made America great. Public officials and a large segment of the public began to question the purposes of education. Antiintellectual sentiment, always latent, was aroused.

Student unrest is more of an excuse than a prime cause for not appropriating funds since the financial crisis affecting education came as early as 1964.

There has been disaffection about relevancy of education and teaching effectiveness, about the educators' attitude that they are the experts; that they know what's best for the students and the public. Recently they have been subjected to serious criticism and challenged by students, legislators, and public. Proposals for evaluation of instructors and attacks on tenure are manifestations of this disaffection. Moreover, the financial crisis is also affecting colleges, public schools in secluded suburban areas, and private, secular, and religious schools that have not had student disorders or have not been involved in civil rights or desegregation issues. While the financial crisis is too deep-seated to be explained away by any simple statement, student activism does rank high as a contributor to the public's negative attitude and bolsters its determination not to support education.

Another cause of public hostility may be that educators did not endear themselves to the students, the public, or the legislators during the years of abundance in education—roughly 1947–1964. They have been accused of losing sight during that period of the students who were being taught and the people who provided the funds.

Overt problems such as faculty militancy and strikes, which

began in the late 1960s, jolted the public. As faculty salaries rose and workloads decreased, the public image of a selfless, dedicated group began to fade. Disclosures that some faculty members were holding two full-time teaching positions contributed to the disfavor. Some have even been accused of arrogance—disdainful of criticism and impatient of suggestion. Spectacular challenges to public sensibility involving employment of extreme leftists and militants heightened the unfavorable reaction and the resistance to increased support of higher education. The politicization of the campus, especially in connection with the Vietnam War, the Kent State and Jackson State tragedies, the Moratorium, Earth Days, and now the supposed threat created by the vote of eighteen-year-olds in college communities, contribute to public displeasure.

While these last activities are usually more common at four-year colleges and universities and are seen by the public as a more serious threat than the less spectacular problems on community college campuses, the latter do suffer to a somewhat lesser degree from the negativist reactions.

The difficulties of gaining funds is compounded by the unavoidable reality that the financial crisis stems in part from seemingly uncontrollable societal forces. Inflation is the most insidious of these since educators can do nothing to retard it, nor can they convince the public that their increased appropriations do not keep pace with the declining purchasing power of the dollar. Included in the inflationary cycle are the high interest rates that reduce the amount of money available for construction. Many districts have had to curtail building plans because the estimates made a year or two before did not allow for spiraling inflation and interest rates. Michigan offers a prime example of the effect of inflation in this area: Between 1966 and 1969, construction costs escalated by approximately 38 percent (according to the minutes of the regular meeting of the Macomb County Community College District, Sept. 16, 1969).

Inflation has forced a few colleges to shorten their calendars and eliminate or reduce summer sessions, evening divisions, and community service programs. More and more educators are seeking funding to compensate for inflation, calling the legislators' attention to the effects on their budgets of the annual 5–7 percent increase in consumer prices. Alfred Flowers, the financial officer of Maricopa

County Community Colleges, Arizona, estimates that since 1962 the purchasing power of state aid for operations went down from $365 per student to $275 and, for capital outlays, from $115 to $88 (1969, pp. 221–224). For a time in 1970, inflation seemed to be under control, increasing only at a moderate pace; interest rates had receded from their high of 1969. Since 1971 the situation has become more serious. Administration efforts to retard the inflationary rise have so far been unsuccessful. Interest rates in mid-1973 exceeded those of the 1969–1970 period. The purchasing power of the dollar has continued downward precipitously (*Newsweek,* July 30, 1973, pp. 50–58).

What community college educators have counted among their greatest accomplishments—attracting large numbers of students—has become a major problem. From 1959 to October 1972 enrollment spurted from 552,000 to more than 2.7 million; the number of colleges increased from 390 to 904 (American Association of Junior Colleges, 1973, pp. 7, 87). The zeal and enthusiasm of educators and students in the 1950s matched that of the nineteenth century, when colleges and universities multiplied at a similar rate. And as was true in the nineteenth century, zeal and enthusiasm flagged as financial realities bore down.

Earlier, financing this huge enterprise caused little concern. Community pride, belief that a college increases the wealth of the community, desire for entertainment and culture, and pressure from parents with college-age children overshadowed concern for financing. The public was assured that the added costs would be absorbed by education's "impact on the national product" and the increase in the "lifetime earnings and working life" of the students (Moynihan, 1966, pp. 75–77); these would presumably provide a wide tax base for subsequent support of the institutions. Education rivaled science in public favor, and educators adjusted to expansion without having to endure the growing pains. The high favor education enjoyed might not have been lost had not other demands for public funds arisen.

National goals such as social security in its various forms, ecological balance, environmental preservation, expanded recreational facilities, and improved transportation—projects that touch many people—became powerful competitors for public funds. Of these, welfare programs garner an increasingly larger amount of public funds and, probably, by the end of the 1970s, will outrank education in the percentage of funds expended. A national survey of sixteen states by *Nation's Business* (1971) reported that welfare costs increased more than fivefold between 1960 and 1970. Nationwide, state general expenditures for education went up 13.7 percent from 1970 to 1971. For welfare they increased by 23.3 percent (U.S. Bureau of the Census, 1972, p. 3).

As welfare draws a larger proportion of public money, resistance to increasing funds for education grows. Moreover, states and cities dependent on the federal government for a large proportion of welfare funds must abide by federal regulations. Attempts in 1971 by California, Indiana, Nebraska, and Nevada to reduce welfare expenditures were stymied by the threat of a cutoff of federal funds. Higher education funds do not have this protection.

The desperate financial situation of state and local governments obligated to provide increasing public services is reflected in the search for new sources of income. States are now resorting to lotteries, a disguised form of taxation with great appeal to many. Of the three lotteries now in operation, those in New Hampshire and New York have been disappointing; only the New Jersey lottery has been rewarding in terms of revenue. Connecticut, Massachusetts, and Pennsylvania have authorized lotteries (*Newsweek,* 1971c). The successful experience in New York with off-track betting (OTB), as opposed to the lottery, may encourage other states to institute similar plans as a source of revenue. However, since 1971 interest in lotteries as a source of revenue has subsided. The only alternatives seem to be to increase the state income tax or impose a city income tax.

Chapter II

✿✿✿✿✿✿✿✿✿✿✿✿✿✿✿✿✿✿✿✿✿✿✿✿✿✿✿✿✿✿✿✿

Internal Practices

Public disaffection, inflation, and competition with other social agencies do not fully explain the strained financial conditions of the colleges. Practices within the institution contribute to both the change of public attitude and the financial crisis. Chief among these is the labor-intensive characteristic of education, which translates into an unusually large proportion of money expended on salaries and other worker benefits. Added to this expense is the drain on finances of ancillary services assumed by or assigned to the colleges. Then there are the increased costs of educating minority and disadvantaged students and other extraordinary expenditures including the startup costs of new colleges, security and insurance, and miscellaneous items requiring matching funds. A discussion of these expenses serves as a prelude to the chapters that follow on the measures colleges are taking to prevent financial disaster.

Education in and out of the classroom is a labor-intensive enterprise in contrast to capital-intensive industries. As now being conducted, it does not lend itself to the introduction of labor-saving devices that achieve greater productivity to offset increasing costs.

Central to education is the instructor. To many the two are synonymous; mention of one evokes the other. Until recently, no one seriously considered a system of education that did not revolve around the instructor. Even the introduction of modern technological devices—television, computer-assisted instruction, system development, programmed learning, autotutorial laboratories—was often accompanied by the assurance that they will not replace the instructor; rather, they are designed to help him do a better job of teaching.

Since instructors hold such a vital place in the educational process, a high salary schedule is considered among the best indicators of the quality of an educational institution (Steiner, 1971). Regardless of the validity of this belief, teacher salaries are the fastest growing item in school budgets. Their step salary schedules permit everyone to advance automatically each year. Also, an instructor may advance to a higher salary by taking courses, doing independent study, and so forth. Additional increases are awarded for further degrees and professional licenses. The whole structure is based on time in service and effort outside the classroom, not on merit in instruction.

Thus, salary schedules necessitate an annual budget increment. Theoretically, the number of new teachers at the low end of the salary schedule balances the number of retiring teachers at the high end. In practice, however, the tendency has been for these salary schedules to become weighted on the top side. Formerly, after reaching the top of the salary schedule, an instructor received no more increases, but lately a new feature—longevity increments at ten, twenty, and twenty-five year intervals—has been added. Generous retirement benefits add to the costs of education.

Another principle tenaciously held, even though it is contrary to available research findings (Dubin and Taveggia, 1968, p. 10), is that a low teaching load is an indicator of quality education.

Since the end of World War II, as salaries have gone up, teaching loads, a measure of productivity, have gone down from twenty contact, or classroom, hours to fifteen and, in some places, to twelve (Carnegie Commission on Higher Education, 1972, p. 69). Administrators find it increasingly difficult to get faculty to perform nonclassroom services without giving them released time or extra compensation, sometimes both. Formerly, this practice was confined mainly to physical education instructors for their coaching assignments; today theater arts, journalism, music, speech, and other instructors who engage in extraclassroom activities demand and receive similar reimbursement.

Fringe benefits, increasing each year, also have an effect on budgets. The most common are sabbaticals, sick leave, bereavement and emergency leaves with pay, health and insurance benefits, expenses for attendance at professional meetings, tuition waivers for dependents, payment of full or part tuition for graduate school courses, and lump-sum payments at retirement for unused sick-leave pay. Medical, dental, and insurance benefits often accrue to dependents. The reproduction rate of fringe benefits alarms some auditors because they "are often tucked away in a little noticed corner of the budget labeled fixed charges" (*Los Angeles Times,* 1970). Fringe benefits increase salary expenditures by at least 8–12 percent.

Retirement benefits in education and in other public employment are more liberal than (in some places twice as high as) those in private industry. Teachers in New York City may retire after twenty years at half their final salaries. The average costs, now 8 percent of payroll funds, will, if benefits continue to be liberalized, rise to at least 11 percent by 1978.

This increase in salaries however, is part of the new style in business, industry, and government, with which educators are attempting to gain parity. It would be unrealistic to expect them to lag behind, remaining untouched by the trend toward a shorter workweek, fringe benefits, and higher pay. On the whole, faculty salaries and fringe benefits account for 40–60 percent of the budget, making the instructor "the most expensive input of the educational enterprise and . . . the heart of the financial crisis" (Coombs, 1968, p. 34). Especially where collective bargaining is employed, faculty salaries rise quickly and teaching loads are lightened.

Collective bargaining is spreading at a modest rate among

community colleges and other two-year postsecondary institutions. As of April 1973 almost 200 of the 866 institutions listed in the *AACJC Directory* were covered by collecting bargaining agreements. These institutions were distributed among sixteen states and the District of Columbia. The latest addition to the group are the twenty-three Minnesota colleges covered by a single contract (*Chronicle of Higher Education,* April 30, 1973, p. 4). They constitute almost half of the fifty-one colleges added to this group since October 1972, when 147 were reported (*Chronicle of Higher Education,* Oct. 2, 1972, p. 1). Pressure for permissive legislation is growing in other states. The threat of collective bargaining or the desire to forestall it often leads colleges to match the benefits of faculty covered by contracts.

Most of the contracts include detailed sections on salaries and workloads. Instructors often scorn administrators' preoccupation with faculty productivity as measured by the number of classroom contact hours and students in a class, yet these two items are often minutely described in contracts negotiated by their representatives. Unions and other faculty groups have not been noted for making concessions on these two points without a struggle, sometimes bitter, and after substantial concessions whose future consequences may come to plague employers. Teacher unions may be forced by legislative action, strong public pressure, or threat of a shutdown to make concessions leading to higher productivity. This might be accomplished through increased workloads in the classroom or the introduction of new technologies that might change the role of the instructor to a manager of a team of paraprofessionals and a laboratory of electronic equipment and prepackaged learning materials. With a surplus of candidates for teaching positions, the unions may be even more reluctant to agree to changes that will increase that surplus. They will argue that education has a responsibility and opportunity to improve teaching and relieve the unemployment crisis, hiring more instructors rather than fewer.

Although administrators and nonprofessional employees absorb a smaller proportion of the educational resources than faculty, they also contribute to the financial crisis. Administrative salaries have risen, workloads have been reduced, fringe benefits have multiplied, and positions have proliferated. As community colleges have become more like senior colleges, their organizational pattern has taken on the same complex characteristics in nomenclature and number of positions. President, vice-presidents, deans, assistant deans, coordinators, and counselors have replaced the simple, older pattern of principal, dean of men, dean of women, registrar, and counselor. Secretaries, clerks, maintenance personnel, technicians, laboratory assistants, readers, and tutors have also become more numerous.

College administrators are also the targets of sharp barbs for being preoccupied with their perquisites, elegant offices, and cafeterias; creating expensive public relations divisions; and allowing the colleges to become topheavy with established functionaries. In the absence of norms, such criticism is difficult to evaluate, but because it comes from public officials as well as from teacher groups, it is difficult to ignore. A further charge made against administrators is that their involvement in outside activities, such as accrediting associations, professional organizations, service and community clubs, consultantships, and speaking engagements, makes it necessary to add backup personnel to take care of what should be their campus duties. Some administrators spend the equivalent of one month a year on such assignments. More than one college president has candidly admitted to his colleagues certain feelings of guilt for spending as much as a fifth to a quarter of his time in noncampus activities.

Administrative overhead is also increased by the use of consultants—a practice that flourishes even as the number of administrators increases. College administrators seem to find it more and more necessary to call on other administrators, university professors, and management firms for almost every kind of advice—from recommendations on what forms to use to what kind of multicampus organization to adopt. The causes for this rising use of consultants include changes in administrative and instructional practices, development of new programs, availability of federal and foundation funds, requirements of accrediting associations, inexperience of administrators, and the tendency of governing boards to seek impartial recommendations before approving expensive or controversial items. In small colleges, consultants often take the place of permanent staff. Whatever the reason, in the overall budget the accumulation of this and other small items has an upward push.

Much of the increase in nonteaching personnel results from the increase in enrollment and new or expanded functions and services. The increase in average size of colleges from five hundred to two thousand students necessitates larger campuses and more building space, which in turn create the need for more personnel.

Concomitantly, expenditures for capital improvements add to the financial problems. Buildings require large sums of money for construction and maintenance. In the search for a solution to the financial crisis, suggestions for efficient use of buildings rank in importance just below those for increased faculty productivity.

New or expanded functions of the colleges such as community services, career education programs, special programs for disadvantaged and minority students, financial aid, health services, and counseling accompany the increases in enrollment. Instructional innovation generates experiments, new teaching methods, and technical devices that often cost more money and usually increase the unit cost of education. Some of this proliferation is internally induced; most comes from outside the institution—from the legislature, federal agencies, foundations, higher education institutions, or professional associations. For instance, it is an unusual accrediting committee that does not recommend that a college provide new services for students or community, additions to the administrative staff, released time to faculty for experimentation, or a research and development unit for the staff. Another frequent recommendation encourages the college to use its taxing authority, if it has any left, or to seek an increase in tax rate or bonding capacity from the electorate. Thus, additional expense is an almost inevitable result of an accrediting committee examination.

As a consequence of their own commitment and of state and national policy, community colleges have attempted to increase, in number and percentage, the enrollment of minority students. To be successful, they must engage in active recruiting, create special learning divisions, and set aside funds for various forms of financial aid—remission of tuition, direct grants, loans, work-study opportunities, placement services, health care, and occasionally free meals and textbooks. In the new learning divisions, additional funds are naturally needed for supervision, student tutors, paraprofessionals, and special teaching devices. Special programs thus increase per capita cost.

Colleges, by virtue of the addition of community to their title, believe that they have the responsibility to assume community functions. Many colleges are creating a division of community services with a high-level administrator and supporting personnel. In a survey of 900 colleges in 1970, 852 reported that they had community service programs, and 486 had assigned staff members to them on a full-time basis (*Developing Junior Colleges,* 1971).

Though they cannot be considered services, campus law enforcement and crime prevention also add to the financial burden. Bombings and bomb scares, incendiarism, window-breaking, vandalism, assault on personnel, and other lawless acts are forcing colleges to create law enforcement departments and to improve security and fire protection devices. Insurance rates have become almost prohibitive for some colleges. Frequent theft of equipment creates innumerable difficulties and inconveniences, as well as monetary loss. Of the security measures that have become imperative, the most costly is the law enforcement department. Whereas formerly one or two watchmen sufficed for protection, now three to ten or more highly paid, deputized officers are being added to college staffs. Few colleges have been able to avoid this additional expense.

Federal funds also contribute to the proliferation of services and activities. Most colleges retain a staff officer whose principal duty is to keep the college informed of federal fund sources and prepare requests for them. Although these funds are minor in relation to the total budget, administrators are willing to spend time and money to seek them out. These funds may also impose a future financial burden on the college, when financing the service that a grant has started with seed money becomes the full responsibility of the college. Colleges that eagerly accepted funds for foreign language laboratories, planetariums, and other facilities discovered that the upkeep was another drain on their resources (Koltai, 1967, pp. 117–123).

These comments are made not as an argument against federal aid but to call attention to the fact that federal aid contributes to the financial problems of the colleges, especially when educators

fail to consider the consequences of obligations imposed by grants on their present or future budgets. As I point out later federal aid for vocational and developmental education, construction of buildings, and student aid is almost indispensable for most colleges.

Since "experiments in higher education never fail," they often "set down roots—faculty and building space" (*Newsweek,* 1971a, p. 63). Also discouraging is that "studies on the relative effectiveness of different instructional techniques demonstrate that, at least as judged by teacher evaluation in the form of course grades and examination scores, any one instructional technique is neither better or worse than any other" (Brightman, 1971, p. 98).

Finally, the prevalence of small classes in new colleges is one of the most serious factors in increasing the cost of education. It is not unusual to find classes with fewer than five students.

This review of the greatest financial crisis in the history of community colleges sounds a note of pessimism for the future. The 1970s do not promise any surcease from the financial problems of the 1960s. The painful experiences thus far in this decade offer little hope for improvement in the next five years. In the 1960s educators ignored critics who questioned their optimistic assumptions about the strength of the educational pedestal. Today some critics attribute a large share of the crisis to the educators themselves, who are alleged to be "probably the worst example in the governmental area of slipshod money-husbandry" (*Los Angeles Times,* 1971b, p. 29). Retrenching almost disappeared from their habits, which may explain why they find the process so painful today and why they are so reluctant to accept its necessity.

One of the serious consequences is that the role of education in our society is being questioned as never before. Societal expectations, raised by the exuberant claims of the capacity of education to bring the good life, have not been fulfilled.

Chapter III

꽃꽃꽃꽃꽃꽃꽃꽃꽃꽃꽃꽃꽃꽃꽃꽃꽃꽃꽃꽃꽃꽃꽃꽃꽃꽃꽃꽃

How Colleges Are
Financed

Community college educators are convinced that the financial
crisis will be resolved primarily by an increase in revenues. They
are exerting their major efforts on all possible sources—local, state,
and federal; students; and private donations. Through state and
national associations they maintain observers and lobbyists in state
capitals and in Washington, D.C.; they carry on state and local
campaigns to secure approval of property tax overrides and capital-
outlay (bond) proposals. Occasionally they must counter efforts to

limit tax rates and other financial measures they consider detrimental to education.

On committees, commissions, and task forces they provide data to support their contention that education should have a larger share of financial resources. They plead annually with governors and legislators to increase state appropriations. Some critics claim that educators have one of the largest and most effective pressure groups in the state capitals. If they do, their accomplishments do not match their strength.

State subsidies, tuition and fees, and property taxes are the three major sources of revenue. Federal funding is increasing for vocational programs, facilities, and student assistance through grants and loans, but its total still represents a small fraction of the income of the college. Even more miniscule are the private and miscellaneous sources. Most locally controlled colleges depend on the three major sources; with few exceptions, state-controlled colleges do not have recourse to property taxes. For both groups, these sources account for 90–95 percent of their income.

The sources of revenue and the relative amount received from each are intimately connected with the financial crisis. Educators probably give as much attention to these as to all other facets of the crisis. Many attribute the financial crisis to the failure of local, state, or federal governments to assume their proper responsibility to provide adequate funds for education. Tuition is considered a last resort, because it may be self-defeating if it gets too high.

Funds for colleges are classified broadly as operating and capital outlay. The former are used in the operation of the college. Occasionally, they may be used for capital-outlay expenditures. Capital-outlay funds are used only for capital-outlay projects—purchase of land, construction, and equipment purchase or replacement. Another distinction between the two is that operating funds are limited to the year or biennium for which they were appropriated. Unused funds at the end of the budget period revert to the general fund for reapportioning the following year. Capital-outlay revenues are retained until the project for which they were granted is completed. A third difference is that expenditures for capital outlay ordinarily do not enter into the calculations of per capita cost of operation. As is described more fully in Chapter Twelve, per capita cost is derived by dividing the total expenditures for operation by the number of full-time students.

A study of capital-outlay and current-operating sources of income in fifteen southern states for 1970–1971 showed that the states received $118 million for capital outlay compared with $462 million for current operations. The percentage distribution from the various sources of funds were: for capital outlay—14.8 (federal), 39.4 (state), 42.1 (local), 0.9 (student), 2.8 (other); for current operation—7.5 (federal), 56.4 (state), 15.2 (local), 18.9 (student), 2.0 (other) (Spencer, 1972a, 1972b).

Capital-outlay funds are usually derived by lump-sum allocations from state bond issues, and in a few cases in which colleges adopt a pay as you go policy, from the regular revenues. State-controlled colleges receive most of their capital-outlay funds from the state. Usually the amount received from the federal government is subtracted from the state allocation. Locally supported colleges receive from the state as much as 75 percent or as little as nothing. The balance needed comes from bond issues, general funds, and federal funds. In the study reported above, federal funds supplied 58 percent of the capital outlay funds for the Arkansas colleges. Kentucky and Maryland reported no federal funds.

The sources of operating income are discussed fully in the next chapter.

Chapter IV

Patterns of
State Support

Several patterns of state subvention for community colleges exist varying from no support; shared effort with local community support; to full support minus tuition and/or federal funds. The patterns fall into three classifications: fixed amount per full-time student; proportionate amount of cost of operations per full-time student; and full state support. Since the tendency in current legislation and practice is to incorporate elements of the first two, some-

19

times completely obscuring the distinction between them, they will be treated together.

Under the original formula pattern—a carryover from the time when colleges were part of the public school system—the state allocated a fixed amount per full-time student, credit, or attendance hour, sometimes providing an equalization formula to help poor districts maintain a minimally adequate program. Formulas for state support are based on full-time student equivalent (FTSE), full-time equivalent enrollment (FTEE), fiscal year-equated student (FYES), full-time equivalent (FTE) which uses credit hour as the unit, or average daily attendance (ADA) which uses attendance hour as the unit. All these terms refer to units of measurement for the purpose of allocating state funds and for comparing enrollments. In practice FTE is the most commonly used abbreviation to represent full-time student equivalents as distinct from student head count, which does not indicate how many units or credit hours are represented by the statistic.

Reimbursement is usually based on current enrollment rather than that of the previous year. One credit hour may mean more than one attendance hour, especially in technical, vocational, and laboratory courses. Some formulas use twenty-four credit hours as a full-time student equivalent, others use thirty, and Michigan uses thirty-one. Illinois uses a flat grant per credit hour. The census or enrollment-count date is usually between the second and fourth week of the semester or quarter. Another requirement specifies that the academic year must consist of a minimum number of weeks, days of instruction, or days that colleges are in session, usually fixed at 36, 150, and 175, respectively.

Appearing more frequently in state-aid formulas are requirements that faculty be assigned a minimum number of weekly classroom teaching hours, student contact hours, a specific student-to-teacher ratio, or a combination of these. California requires that 50 percent of the operating budget be spent on classroom teachers' salaries. Other restrictions, not always related to financing, are imposed.

Directly or indirectly, the state-support formulas specify the programs or courses and sometimes the kind of student (resident, adult) who will be subsidized, thereby attempting to prevent duplication of programs and clientele among the various segments of education. Almost universally, state formulas provide higher rates of reimbursement for technical-vocational programs than for academic programs, to offset their higher costs and to encourage colleges to offer more of them. Additional funds are also usually provided for remedial programs and disadvantaged students.

Courses or programs subsidized by private, federal, or special state appropriations receive reduced or no support under state formulas. Also excluded from reimbursement are out-of-state students and others whose tuition payments approximate the full cost of instruction.

Some formulas provide graduated payments based on enrollment, with or without differentiation based on the kind of program. Others, like the Michigan Formula for 1971–1972, combine size of enrollment and program criteria as illustrated in Table 1.

Missouri, New York, and Pennsylvania combine a percentage of the operating costs not to exceed a fixed sum per FTE as criteria in allocating state aid. For example, New York provides aid equal to one-third the cost of instruction with a maximum of $518, but colleges implementing a full opportunity program may receive 40 percent of the operating budget, with a maximum of $621. Other aid is provided for colleges enrolling disadvantaged students in proportion to the number of disadvantaged in the population (State University of New York, 1972, pp. 9–13).

In a period of rising costs, the fixed-formula pattern results in a reduction of the share of expenditures taken by the state and an increase in the contribution by the local district and in tuition charges. Although upward adjustments in state aid are made, they hardly keep pace with rising costs. In a state where aid has not been adjusted, such as Arizona where no increases were made from 1962 to 1972, the effect on local taxes and tuition is compounded. Sometimes the legislature fails to provide sufficient funds for all the students who wish to enroll; then, equalization aid or foundation aid is reduced.

In apportioning funds some states try to equalize or bring income up to a certain level considered necessary to conduct a reasonably adequate instructional program. Equalization aid, in addition to the regular allotment, is provided to colleges with special prob-

Table 1.
FORMULA CRITERIA FOR STATE AID

	Rate per FYES (31 credit hours)		
	Liberal Arts, Commerce, and Business	Vocational-Technical	Health
A. Colleges with enrollment of at least 4,000 FYES	$537	$788	$846
B. Colleges with enrollment of at least 1,000 FYES but less than 4,000 FYES	$600	$788	$846
C. Colleges with enrollment of less than 1,000 FYES	$701	$788	$846

Source: State of Michigan, 1971, Section 9C.

lems created by small enrollment, location in a low socioeconomic or depressed area, or enrollment of a large number of disadvantaged students. This aid may be granted in a fixed sum or graduated according to enrollment, number of disadvantaged students, or wealth of district as measured by income statistics or by assessed valuation of property. The ultimate of equalization aid is exemplified by the State Community College of East St. Louis, located in a heavily segregated, poor economic area of Illinois. Whereas all the other districts in the state must levy a property tax, the East St. Louis College receives full state support of almost two million dollars. No property tax is levied and no tuition is charged. For seven other colleges, the total equalization grants amounted to slightly more than one million dollars (Office of Research, Management Information Systems and Legislation, pp. 8, 12). As noted above, the formula pattern used in New York State has a built-in equalization factor for colleges implementing a full opportunity program and for those enrolling disadvantaged students in proportion to their number in the population. The Michigan formula also incorporates size of enrollment in its formula.

However, more states are increasing their aid to community colleges and in some cases allot even more than to state colleges and universities. With few exceptions, this generalization applies to locally supported as well as state-supported colleges.

The motives for priority funding for two-year colleges are mixed. But basic to this apparently high priority is the fact that they will occupy the same role economically, politically, and socially in the next two decades as the elementary schools did during the 1900s, when immigrants formed a large percentage of the population. There is an additional correlation with earlier times when the country was concerned about child labor. Today, concern over the social and economic disabilities of minority and disadvantaged youth, plus the ability to operate with a much smaller proportion of the population in the work force than formerly, explains in part the interest of the state and federal governments in the two-year institutions. Costs and open access are two other factors in favor of community colleges at state capitals. A few university educators question the claim of lower cost, insisting that their lower-division costs are comparable to or lower than those of the community colleges. By pointing to large classes and use of teaching assistants, they sometimes make a strong case. But legislators are not impressed by such claims. On open access, there is no disagreement. In fact, many university educators welcome community colleges because it makes it possible for them to continue selective admissions. In a few states, Indiana for example, university educators continue to oppose the establishment of community colleges, fearing that adequate state funds will become more difficult to obtain if they have to share them.

Locally, communities—especially those that are not large enough to support a four-year college or university—go to great pains and expense to establish two-year colleges probably for pride, economics, and to keep their youth from emigrating to the cities.

From a tabulation in the *Chronicle of Higher Education,*

(Feb. 7, 1972, p. 1; Apr. 10, 1972, p. 6) community colleges in twenty-seven states, plus the City University of New York system, received a higher percentage of state appropriations for 1972–1974 than the total appropriated for all of higher education; colleges in six states received a lower percentage, and for colleges in seventeen states there was either no change or it was not possible to determine the relative standing.

A discussion of state-aid patterns confined to percentages or unit allocations fails to explain the crisis in college and state finances. Because they are small, unit allocations and percentages do not indicate the magnitude of appropriations made by the states or the even greater sums colleges estimate they need to carry on adequate educational programs. Governors and legislatures also use unit allocations and percentages in their calculations, but when making appropriations they must come up with dollars.

Fifteen southern and border states reported state allocations of $260.86 million, or 56 percent of the total sources of income for 1970–1971. The average for the top five states of this group was $194 million, or 58.4 percent of the total sources of income (Spencer, 1972b). For the same year California appropriated $153.44 million; Illinois, $47.66 million; Michigan, $43.37 million; Colorado, $25.98 million; and Oregon, $13.56 million. For these twenty states alone the total approaches half a billion dollars.

These expenditures have risen constantly. In Illinois, for example, state apportionments (not including special appropriations) have been $34.75, $41.93, and $48.20 million for the three years beginning 1969–1970 (Illinois Junior College Board, 1972a, p. 2). For the same period the California allocations have been $126.76, $153.44, and $176.28 million (telephone interview with A. L. McPherran, May 15, 1972). The Oregon allocations were $11.58, $13.56, and $18.50 million during the same time interval (Oregon Board of Education, 1971, p. 3).

Formula-pattern states also receive various amounts of state aid for capital outlay purposes. Arizona allocates $115 per FTE each year. In Illinois a district may receive up to 75 percent for construction of buildings and site improvement, but the local district must contribute at least 25 percent of the total cost, excluding federal funds (Martin and Thornblad, 1970, p. 10). Pennsylvania provides 50 percent. Arney points out that while very little or no state aid is provided in Missouri, Montana, New Mexico, North Dakota, and Texas, Kansas colleges are unique among locally supported colleges in receiving full state aid for capital outlay (1970, p. 30). In California the aid is awarded on a matching basis formula. New York provides up to one-half the amount approved by the State University trustees (State University of New York, 1972).

A study made by Spencer (1972a) showed state allocations of $46.68 million for nine states. In the top five states alone, the allocations were $38.45 million. Since capital outlay allocations are not made as regularly as those for operating expenditures, it is more difficult to estimate the yearly expenditures. The total probably is about one-fourth that for operating expenditures.

This sampling shows that states have made large and increasing contributions to the operating income of the community colleges. Despite the concern of governors and legislators over the increasing demands for state appropriations and despite the talk about restricting expenditures, community colleges continue to receive fair to generous treatment. But, as we have noted, few administrators consider state aid adequate for financing the colleges. It seems certain that, in the future, states will assume a larger share of the financing of community colleges, but probably not to the extent considered necessary by educators.

Full state support (minus tuition) is slowly replacing the formula patterns of locally supported colleges. Three categories of colleges receiving full support exist: those whose status is coordinate with state colleges and universities but whose budget is separate; those operated as autonomous units of state college and university systems under a budget administered by the senior institution; and branches or satellite campuses of state colleges or universities.

In the first group are the community colleges in Colorado, Connecticut, Delaware, Florida, Massachusetts, Minnesota, Oklahoma, and Virginia. Colorado, Massachusetts, and Oklahoma also have locally supported colleges. In establishing its system of community colleges, Massachusetts withdrew state support from colleges that chose not to enter the system. Originally two colleges took that option, but have since requested to join the state system (Dwyer, 1972). Colorado also gave existing colleges the option of joining the state system, and by 1971 all but three did so. However, unlike the Massachusetts colleges, the three holdouts are not penalized by withdrawal of state support.

The university-affiliated colleges of Alaska, Georgia, Hawaii, and Kentucky form essentially an autonomous group; they are not branch or satellite campuses. On the other hand, university-affiliated two-year colleges in North Dakota, Ohio, Pennsylvania, South Carolina, Virginia, West Virginia, and other states, are branch or satellite campuses that often grow into four-year colleges. However, their status is not always clearcut; many opt for regional accreditation as two-year or community colleges.

The characteristic common to all these colleges is that they are state-supported rather than locally supported. In contrast, in the New York system, the university-affiliated community colleges are locally controlled and supported in part by local taxes. The system exemplifies the inconsistency in patterns of state support for higher education.

Allocations of funds to state-supported colleges are usually based on student enrollment projections for the year or biennium. Appropriations may also be based on a faculty-student ratio or on need as expressed in the requests made at each legislative session. Florida, which in 1971 joined the states providing full support, introduced a new formula based on the product of the cost ratio of a discipline (based on state average cost for the previous year), a unitary value, and the projected FTE. In a hypothetical example the allocation for X College is determined as shown in Table 2.

With few exceptions, colleges in the state systems receive all capital outlay funds from the state. However, local governmental units in many states must provide the land and share some costs related to construction. In Washington the state may issue revenue bonds based on 60 percent of tuition income, while the local district may do the same based on 40 percent of tuition. Oklahoma requires that the local community in which a state junior college is to be established donate to the state a suitable site for the college. In Georgia, the development of a new college is contingent upon the local political division's providing funds for a site for construction and equipping the initial buildings.

The future points to full state support of community colleges,

Table 2.
FORMULA CRITERIA FOR STATE AID (Florida)

Cost Ratio of Discipline × Unitary = Discipline Cost × FTE
= Amount Allocated

Biological Study	1.4 × $950 = $1,330	× 100 = $133,000
Agriculture	1.5 × $950 = $1,425	× 50 = $ 71,250
Enrichment	0.9 × $950 = $ 855	× 50 = $ 42,750
	Total Allocations	$247,000

Source: Current, 1972, pp. 2, 3.

but a large number of administrators still prefer the local-state support system. Those in locally supported colleges believe they have more assurance of adequate support from the property tax plus a state allocation than from full state support; that state appropriations on a formula pattern are more likely to be uniformly allocated than appropriations subject to legislative approval at each budget session; and that they are less subject to state control in their expenditures of funds.

A good deal of emotion revolves around the issue of state support. Much of it is associated with the issue of local versus state control. Community college educators in locally controlled colleges believe they have more freedom in the operation of their colleges than do those in state-controlled colleges. There is some justification for this belief. Colleges that originally developed from the local school systems did retain a good deal of control. Colleges that developed from state commissions and agencies have had to contend with more control. Florida colleges, for example, which have always received more state support, also receive more direction from the state capital than do California colleges. But this difference is not as great as formerly. As colleges asked for and received more state aid, they became subject to more state control. A direct relationship is difficult to establish, probably both developed concurrently. However, the evidence is that local control is giving way to state control. State commissions or boards for community colleges are becoming as common in locally supported as in state-supported states. Complaints of too much regulation are heard in California and Illinois as in states which provide support. The issue is complicated by the growth of subsystems with two to eight colleges. For these colleges, most of which are locally supported, state control may be less of a problem than control by the local district administration.

Some colleges prefer local control because it enables them to maintain segregated (white) colleges, particularly in states with large cities surrounded by suburbs. The suburban colleges try by one means or another to keep the low socioeconomic and minority high school graduates from enrolling, an advantage that will disappear as soon as the eighteen-year-olds acquire all the rights of adulthood.

In a few instances in Colorado and Massachusetts, community colleges have chosen to stay out of the state-controlled system, even though in Massachusetts the two colleges that did so received no state aid. In May 1973, Oregon voters rejected a proposal that would have shifted 95 percent of all support for public schools to the state and eliminated nearly all property taxes. Voters feared that full state funding would mean loss of local control.

Some administrators feel that they can get more money from the combination of local taxes and state subventions than from either source alone. This was the reason the president of state-supported Tulsa Junior College appealed for permission to revert to local support. But this is an exceptional situation. This argument overlooks the existence or development of formula patterns in the distribution of funds in state-supported colleges. The Florida formula, with its introduction of a cost ratio factor for each discipline, is one of the more imaginative efforts in allocating funds among the colleges. In the long run the logic of a uniform method of funding all higher education institutions, expediency, and property-tax reform will have more influence on the patterns of support than rhetoric or argument.

Chapter V

❀❀❀❀❀❀❀❀❀❀❀❀❀❀❀❀❀❀❀❀❀❀❀❀❀❀❀❀❀

Property Taxes

Property taxes are a major source of revenue for colleges in all but a dozen states. For some it is the major source. Locally supported colleges dependent on the property tax for some of their funds enroll more than two-thirds of all community and junior college students.

Although property taxes are set by local boards of trustees, legislatures are deeply involved with the kind and amount of levy that may be made on property. Local boards must contend with an assortment of constitutional and legislative prescriptions and proscriptions on their taxing powers.

29

The three major property taxes common to most locally supported colleges are: the general-purpose tax, which may be used for any authorized expenditure although it is used mainly for general operations; special-purpose taxes, which are being levied with more frequency; and the capital-outlay tax, which can be used only for buildings and equipment. Among these three sources, the general-purpose tax produces the largest amount of revenue.

Generally, property taxes provide 25–50 percent of the operating revenues. In the case of a few colleges, however, especially those with no or low tuition, this tax is the principal source of revenue, accounting for 60 percent or more of the total funds.

Legislatures set minimum or maximum rates that may be levied on property. California, for instance, has a maximum of $0.38 per $100 of assessed valuation, which may be increased only by a majority vote of the electorate or special legislative action. In Michigan a college district loses a specified proportion of state funds if it fails to levy a one-mill-per-dollar tax on property. The one-mill rate is also a maximum that may be increased only by a majority vote of the electorate.

The practice of limiting the tax rate leads to various devices to circumvent it with or without the approval of the legislature or electorate. New special taxing districts can be created or permissive tax overrides authorized by the legislature. Besides the general-purpose tax rate, separate rates may be set up for community services, adult education, retirement, social security, health and welfare benefits, and construction—special purposes. Because some of these tax rates, such as those for retirement and debt service, have no ceiling, the hard-pressed trustees and administrators shift as much of the overhead to them as they can justify.

The capital-outlay tax, on the other hand, is more permanent; it is actually a special-purpose tax of long standing. In most states it is restricted to a percentage of the assessed valuation of property, usually not more than five percent. In Michigan the five-mill-per-dollar levy is continuous, while in California the levy varies because the tax rate is computed on the basis of the amount necessary to meet interest and bond redemptions. Consequently, districts with no outstanding bonds will have no capital-outlay tax rate.

In recent years the California general-purpose and other tax rates have ranged from $0.37 to $1.24 with a median of $0.67 (Coast Community College District, 1972). In Illinois the range has been $0.10 to $0.39 with a median of $0.20 (Office of Research, Management Information Systems and Legislation, 1972, p. 18). In Oregon the median tax rate for 1971–1972 was $1.49 with a low of $0.75 and a high of $2.23 (Oregon Community College Assn., 1972, p. 62).

Along with the size of the tax rate, income is influenced by the assessed valuation of the property. Rising valuations during the last ten years have provided a modest increase in revenues to locally controlled colleges, but the increase has not matched the rise in costs.

The disparity between the rate of increase in assessed valuation and high enrollments may be illustrated by examples from California, Illinois, and Michigan. In one California district during 1968–1969 and 1970–1971, assessed valuation increased by less than 5 percent while enrollment went up more than 12 percent (Coast District, 1969–1971). Unless a district could increase its tax rate, it had to seek more support from the state or curtail its program or enrollment, or both. The Illinois situation for 1969–1971 was similar. Assessed valuation increased slightly more than 15 percent, while enrollment rose almost 27 percent (Office of Research, Management Information Systems and Legislation, 1972, pp. 13, 14, 15).

In a period of static or declining enrollment, or in a rapidly expanding economy in which assessed valuation rises correspondingly, the situation is reversed. Until 1970, Oakland Community College in Michigan experienced unusually high year-to-year enrollment increases while assessed valuations went up at a more gradual rate. However, a change for the better took place in 1970–1971 when enrollment increased only 10 percent while assessed valuation increased 18 percent. Table 3 illustrates the relationship between the relative rates of increase for the period 1965–1966 through 1970–1971. If colleges survive for a few more years, it is possible that a centain amount of relief may be obtained from this source if enrollments stabilize or fall.

Besides the general financial stringency affecting colleges everywhere, the financial problems of locally supported community

Table 3.
ASSESSED VALUATION AND FULL-TIME
EQUIVALENT ENROLLMENTS, 1965–1966 to 1970–1971

Fiscal Year	Assessed Valuation (thousands)	Yearly Increase Per Cent	FTE[a]	Yearly Increase Per Cent
1965–1966	$2,447,383		2,469	
1966–1967	$2,673,680	9	2,754	12
1967–1968	$3,017,000	13	4,080	45
1968–1969	$3,434,600	14	6,801	67
1969–1970	$3,990,759	16	8,767	29
1970–1971 (*Estimated*)	$4,698,236	18	9,676	10

[a] 31 credit hours = 1 FTE.
Source: Oakland Community College, 1970.

colleges are compounded by inequities in the tax bases and by adherence to the concept of local control. These problems are more prevalent among the states that pioneered in the development of the colleges than among those that have established colleges in more recent years on a statewide basis, supported in large part by state funds.

California, Illinois, Iowa, Michigan, Missouri, and Texas are experiencing these additional problems. The situation in Texas is indicative of the others. The community college districts cover about 10 percent of the geographical area and one-third of the taxable wealth. Yet, the colleges in these districts enroll students from 251 of the 254 counties. Although an out-of-district fee is imposed, it is "far less than the proportion that in-district property owners pay." In addition to supporting their local colleges, these taxpayers are assessed (along with other taxpayers) for the support of the building program of seventeen of the twenty-two state colleges. A third inequity is that some urban centers like Austin, Houston, and Port Arthur-Beaumont have senior colleges entirely supported by the state; some of these were originally two-year colleges (Texas Research League, 1970, p. 12).

The California legislature has resolved most of the geographical inequities mentioned in two steps. First, it permits college districts to bill the cost of education plus a seat charge to the county of residence of a student from an area not operating a community college. Second, it requires every area not in a community college district to form one or to annex to an adjoining district. The result is that currently only a very few areas are not in a community college district. By 1974 all areas must be.

Illinois has also used this means of coercion on non-junior college areas. Recent legislation requires all non-junior college territory to annex to an existing district or form a new district if the area can meet the requirements of a 60,000 population and $150 assessed evaluation. In a similar move, Iowa's reorganization of the community college system established districts covering the state.

These laws have not eliminated all inequities, especially those relating to disparities in assessed valuation of property among the various districts. To compensate partially for these disparities, states have enacted equalization formulas, subsidies for colleges with small enrollments, and various grants for colleges with large numbers of minority and disadvantaged students. But the most effective means of eliminating the inequities, and increasing revenues, lies in the adoption of the proposals for a statewide property tax.

The financial strain on local districts is serious enough that the state should assume responsibility for supporting education from Head Start to graduate school, freeing property tax revenue for purposes such as sewers, garbage disposal, fire, and police protection —functions directly related to services rendered to property. Such was a recommendation of the Advisory Commission on Intergovernmental Relations. In his testimony before Congress, the assistant director of the commission (Shannon, 1970) remarked that state takeover would represent a giant step toward equalization of educational opportunity, fix political accountability for educational financing on the governor and state legislature, and eliminate divided responsibility for measurement of student achievement.

The Research and Policy Committee of the Committee for

Economic Development (CED) recommended that "in most states the state government should take over from the local districts a larger share of the financial burden of school . . . [because] the inherent limitations of the property tax . . . are serious obstacles to the flow of funds into education" (Committee for Economic Development, 1967, p. 38).

In addition, the Texas Research League (1970, p. i), recommended that "the state finance the full cost of community colleges, including state assumption of outstanding general obligation bonds, and that public junior colleges be prohibited from levying a property tax." Six years earlier a Governor's Committee on Education Beyond the High School recommended that the state should pay "all junior college institutional costs for all courses approved by the Coordinating Board" (Texas, 1964, p. 48).

The California *Serrano* v. *Priest* decision, along with other judgments rendered in Minnesota, New Jersey, and Texas, have offered dramatic support for the movement to reduce dependence on the property tax as a source of revenue for education. They have questioned or declared unconstitutional its present use for the support of the public schools. The most widely quoted *Serrano* decision declares that "free public schools shall make available to all children equally the abundant gifts of learning." The decision does not attack the property tax as such, but the inequities that result from the presence of high-revenue-producing properties in some districts and their absence in others—differences that the court contended lead to a violation of the 14th Amendment of the federal constitution guaranteeing equal protection of the laws to all persons. The Court added: "To allot more educational dollars to the children of one district than to those of another merely because of the fortuitous presence of such property is to make the quality of a child's education dependent upon the location of private, commercial, and industrial establishments."

The *Serrano* decision is understandably attracting national attention from public school and community college educators, who depend on the property tax as a source of revenue. Although it refers to the elementary and secondary schools, the community colleges will be affected by the ruling, primarily because of the similarity between the financing plan of community colleges and public schools. "The principle that the quality of education may not be a function of wealth" applies wherever property taxes are a source of revenue (Deegan, 1971, p. 1; see also Crowl, 1971).

It will be some time before all the implications of *Serrano* and similar rulings are known. One implication was resolved by the five-to-four United States Supreme Court decision in the Texas *Rodriguez* case. It ruled that property tax reform must come from the state legislative process and not through the federal courts via the Fourteenth Amendent. Since *Serrano* is based on state law (and the Fourteenth Amendment) not in conflict with federal law, it may be upheld or not even be heard by the Supreme Court. Whatever the outcome, property tax reform, seems likely to come through legislative action, a much more laborious process than judicial appeal (*Los Angeles Times,* 1973, Part 1, p. 1).

Property taxes continue to rise wherever educators have the option to raise them. Educators may sympathize with the plight of the property owners, but they feel that their first obligation is to keep the colleges operating at maximum strength. They also resist attempts such as the Michigan proposal for a property tax freeze and the California initiatives to limit the amount of property tax that may be levied.

In the face of so much opposition, why does the property tax persist as a source of revenue for community colleges and public schools? In addition to the often emotional attachment to the principle of local control, the answer lies in the stability, ready identification, and tremendous value of property, which makes collection easy and returns high, and the inability of legislators and governors to agree on substitute sources of revenue. If the legislatures do not find a satisfactory solution for property tax relief, the electorate may force the issue by approving referendum measures to limit the rate and the purposes for which tax funds may be used.

Chapter VI

❀❀❀❀❀❀❀❀❀❀❀❀❀❀❀❀❀❀❀❀❀❀❀❀❀❀❀❀❀

Tuition and Fees

Most colleges resort to tuition and fees to help make up some of the differences between budget requirements and inadequate state and local revenues. Pronouncements that no tuition or low tuition should prevail in the community colleges attract attention, but they have little effect on legislators, governors, trustees, and administrators faced with the necessity of balancing budgets. In the 1970s a reversal of the trend toward tuition and fees as an increasing source of revenue is unlikely. The refusal of the American Association of Community and Junior Colleges Assembly in 1972 to support a request for a no-tuition statement is an indication of how far national leaders have come toward accepting or acquiescing to the position that students should pay part of the cost of instruction.

All colleges classify students for tuition purposes: in-district or resident, out-of-district, and out-of-state or nonresident. The terms are used interchangeably. Occasionally, a fourth classification —foreign—is used. While locally controlled colleges apply all three classifications, state-supported systems use only two—resident and nonresident. A state resident may attend any college in the state. A nonresident usually pays a higher tuition. Likewise, in-district tuition is usually lower than out-of-district and much lower than out-of-state tuition.

A few exceptions occur, however. Often, an out-of-district student's tuition is paid in whole or in part by his district of residence on a charge-back or interdistrict agreement or policy. A few states even have reciprocal arrangements permitting out-of-district and out-of-state students to register on the same basis as in-district or resident students. In California a student must get permission from the college in his home district before he may enroll in a college outside his district. While many colleges classify foreign students simply as out-of-state, they are sometimes required to pay an even higher tuition than students in that category.

Out-of-district tuition is not normally intended to be a source of revenue. Theoretically, it is a device to prevent a district from shifting its educational responsibility to other districts; force an area not in a college district to join or annex to one; or prevent a student from attending a college outside his district except under special circumstances.

Although it was not originally imposed as a source of revenue, the amounts derived from out-of-district tuition can be an important addition to income. In Illinois the total charge-back revenue for all colleges amounted to almost $5 million for the 1969–1970 college year. Of this amount $1.6 million was received from other college districts and $3.23 million came from noncollege districts (Illinois Junior College Board, 1971c).

The revenue from this source runs considerably higher for California, but it has been declining as more noncollege areas are incorporated in existing or new college districts. For the state as a whole, it declined from $15 million in 1964–1965 to $8.7 million in

1970–1971 (California Bureau of Junior College Administration and Finance, 1971).

Charge-back revenue will cease being a source of funds for states with locally controlled colleges as districts eventually cover all the territory of each state. The loss of this income will not be of serious consequence, however, since it will presumably be replaced by property tax proceeds.

An examination of current tuition policies automatically involves some analysis of the practice of charging fees. Colleges generally make a distinction between a fee and tuition, though the terms are sometimes used interchangeably. A fee may be a one-time impost, such as an application or graduation fee; a nuisance or penalty tax for failure to perform some action on time, such as late registration, return of a library book, or taking a late examination; an occasional charge for using a special facility, such as a parking lot, music room, or laboratory; or a service charge for health services or membership dues in the student body association. Some college catalogs list as many as twenty of these charges.

Theoretically, tuition is a charge for instruction, while a fee is a charge for a service only peripherally related to instruction. For certain fees—parking, health, athletics—this distinction is valid, but for others—graduation, matriculation, use of models in art classes, music rooms, laboratory equipment—it is less tenable. Some community college educators prefer the term *fee* to *tuition,* reflecting their uneasiness at the contradiction between the concept of the open door and the practice of charging tuition. The use of *fee* may also be a circumvention of state law that forbids tuition but permits fees.

State legislation on tuition and fees is far from standarized. Where tuition is authorized, colleges may charge only a uniform amount set by state law; be required to charge a minimum; be limited to a fixed-amount maximum or amount not to exceed a proportion of the operating cost of instruction; be permitted or prohibited from remitting tuition; or use tuition funds only for prescribed purposes. Tuition may be expressed as an amount per credit hour, semester, or quarter. The per credit hour charge for a part-time student may be larger than for a full-time student. The legislation on fees is even more varied; where it exists, colleges seem to have more latitude in its interpretation, although even here guidelines are becoming more prescriptive.

In contrast to the comparatively low out-of-district tuition levied by a few locally controlled colleges, the tuition charged out-of-state students is almost universally high and often approximates that charged in independent four-year colleges and universities. They range from about $321 per year in North Carolina to almost $2000 per year in some Illinois colleges.

These high-to-moderate rates are designed to deter out-of-state students from enrolling rather than yield a significant source of revenue—this appears to be successful.

The percentage of enrolled out-of-state students varies from less than 0.5 percent in Illinois; to less than 2 percent for the New York Community Colleges; to an exceptionally high 8 percent in Florida (Illinois Junior College Board, 1971f, Table 10; State University of New York, 1971, p. 3; Florida Department of Education, 1971, p. 137). With few exceptions, the percentage of income derived from out-of-state student tuition is very small, rarely exceeding 2 percent.

As the cost of operating the community colleges mounts, nonresident charges continue to escalate, virtually excluding out-of-state students. Even though educators agree that out-of-state students add to the cultural mix of the student body, help "in pursuing the purpose of a quality higher education for young people" (Hawaii University, 1970, p. 9), and make possible curriculum diversity and economies in small colleges, they are forced to concede that "their school's first responsibility is to provide higher education opportunities for qualified students from the community that supports it" (Arizona State Board of Directors, 1969, p. 3).

In contrast to the relatively small income colleges derive from nondistrict and nonresident students, the income from resident students is a significant source of revenue often equalling or exceeding income from the property tax in locally controlled colleges. During the 1960s, both the percentage of colleges that charged tuition and the amount of tuition increased. In the first year of that decade, 36 percent of community colleges had no tuition; by 1968 the figure was 18 percent. Another way of viewing the change is that the 18 percent of colleges charging $200–500 per year in 1960 became 68 percent in 1968 (Huther, 1971).

The upward tuition trend may be illustrated by the experiences of the locally controlled colleges (plus one state college) in Illinois. From Table 4 it is apparent that tuition in the Illinois colleges has risen steadily. Since 1969–1970 the number of colleges charging $10–15 per credit hour ($300–450 per FTE) has more than doubled from five to thirteen. It is also apparent that once a tuition policy was adopted by a district there was no return to a tuition-free policy. Of eight districts that began with a no-tuition policy, only five have retained it, including the State Community College, financed by state funds. Note the large increase in the number of districts that raised tuition in 1971–1972.

Tuition increases reported for 1972–1973 were not as high as those in 1971–1972. Partly accounting for this slowdown was the higher state income colleges received when the subvention of $15.50 per credit hour was raised to $16.50 and the higher rate of increase of assessed valuation and the lower rate of increase of enrollment experienced by some districts.

Few exceptions exist to this trend toward increasing tuition and greater dependence on tuition and fees as sources of revenue. As in Illinois, rarely does a college (or state) that has initiated tuition revert to a no-tuition policy or reduce tuition. Not including fees, tuition charges of $300–400 are becoming common. By the end of the 1970s, it is reasonably certain that average charges will approach $500, with some colleges imposing as much as $1000.

Also by that time, colleges in California, Chicago, and New York City will have to abandon the fiction of a no-tuition policy and adopt an out-and-out tuition charge, or else continue to increase the open and hidden fees they now impose. In California, the tuition-free policy is being eroded by a variety of laboratory fees of doubtful legality, permissive parking fees, and tuition charges for certain categories of adult students. For example, at least twenty-two districts in Califoria now impose a defined adult fee (Gold, 1972a, p. 5). In January 1972, Governor Nelson Rockefeller warned Mayor John Lindsay that he would not recommend larger state appropriations for the city colleges unless they affiliated with the

Table 4.

Selected Statistics on Semester Credit-Hour Tuition for Resident Students[a]

| | 1966–1967 | 1966–1967 to 1971–1972 | | | | |
		1967–1968	1968–1969	1969–1970	1970–1971	1971–1972
Number of Districts[b]	19	26	32	35	37	37
Number Charging Tuition	13	21	27	28	31	32
For Those Charging Tuition[c]						
Mean	$ 5.55	$5.35	$ 5.70	$ 6.65	$ 7.17	$ 8.20
Median	$ 5.00	$5.00	$ 5.50	$ 6.25	$ 7.00	$ 8.00
Low	$ 2.00	$2.00	$ 2.25	$ 2.25	$ 2.25	$ 2.25
High	$10.50	$8.50	$10.00	$12.50	$12.50	$15.00
Number of Districts Charging $10–15	1	0	1	5	8	15
Number of Decreases	—	2	0	0	0	0
Number of Increases	—	4	6	9	8	14

Source: Illinois Junior College Board, 1971d, p. 27.

[a] Does not include mandatory fees.

[b] Includes State Community College of East St. Louis organized in 1969–1970.

[c] Charges are for one semester credit hour.

State University of New York system, a step which would mean the end of the city's 125-year-old free-tuition policy (*Chronicle of Higher Education*, Jan. 17, 1972, p. 3).

Rockefeller has not relented in his efforts to bring the City University of New York, which includes community colleges, into the state system. His 1973 budget for state aid for New York City colleges was coupled with a provision that the governor appoint half the members of the governing board, a move interpreted as a step in his plan to force tuition on the colleges (Kibbee, 1973).

Eventually, as colleges get accustomed to parking, health service, and adult fees, they become more receptive to others. Administrators are now talking more openly about the possibility of tuition—something rarely discussed less than five years ago. In each of the three systems mentioned, the financial situation is precarious, as evidenced by the yearly pleas of the New York City colleges for more state aid, the large deficit of more than $4 million of the Chicago colleges, and the deficit financing many California colleges are facing.

So grave is the crisis in California that administrators who oppose tuition keep asking the legislature for mandatory student-body fee, a "minimum fee for ancillary services," "an application registration fee," and a $1 penalty for change of program (California Junior College Association, 1971a, pp. 1, 4). Indicative of the justifications offered is a statement prepared by the Executive Director of the California Junior College Association that "The Association's stand against tuition should not, and does not, conflict with the desire to relieve to some extent the local tax burden by promoting a minimal fee for ancillary services, such as recently authorized parking and health service fees. The Association still supports such a concept for the so-called 'student body fee,' provided such a fee could be waived in appropriate circumstances" (Messersmith, 1972, p. 2).

A 1970–1971 survey of fifteen states reported tuition income of $88.1 million, representing 18.9 percent of operation income and 0.9 percent of capital outlay expenditures (Spencer, 1972a, 1972b). From a sampling of 283 public colleges, Peterson found that in 1971 tuition averaged $214, and that the average rise for 1971 over 1970 was estimated to be $18, or a 9 percent increase. But since California, Chicago, Hawaii, and New York City colleges (probably included in the sample) do not charge tuition, the estimate of $214 may not reflect the average of colleges that do (Peterson, 1972, p. 30). An estimate from an HEW publication estimates that tuition and fees have risen from $97 in 1962–1963 to $242 in 1972–1973 (Simon and Grant, 1972, p. 100).

Using the Huther, Peterson, and HEW studies plus the data gathered for this book, the average yearly tuition and fees in 1972 for colleges charging them may be close to $300 per FTE. This estimate may seem high, but not if all voluntary and compulsory fees are included.

From this selected review of tuition and fee trends it is apparent that, as in the other segments of higher education, tuition and fees are becoming an important source of revenue for the community colleges. Making estimates of tuition and fees as a percentage of the total budget is complicated by methods of reporting and classification. Colleges report no tuition even when they require students to pay fees of a sizable amount. In states where tuition is charged, but restricted, the law does not always prevent colleges from increasing revenue by imposing fees for noninstitutional purposes. For example, for the period 1964–1970, Harrisburg Area Community College received 44.1 percent of its revenue from tuition and fees, yet Pennsylvania limits tuition to one-third of the operating costs (Harrisburg Area Community College, 1970).

The pattern of state legislation leads to the conclusion that, although governors and legislators look on tuition as an important source of revenue, they are still reluctant to shift more than one-third of the cost of instruction to the students. Until now increased state aid to community colleges has helped keep tuition within bounds.

It is also probable that tuition will continue to be much lower in the community colleges than in the state colleges and universities. Two reasons account for this; first, in their attempts to maintain open access to higher education, states are interpreting that benefit to mean open access to the community college, which in turn implies no or low-tuition. Second, states are trying to control enrollments in the more costly state colleges and universities by diverting first-time freshmen to the community colleges (*Higher*

Education in the States, 1972, p. 58)'. Low tuition is a major inducement to students, along with less selective entrance requirements.

A variety of influences will affect the future tuition pattern in the community colleges. The first is the amendment granting eighteen-year-olds the right to vote. An immediate effect of the legislation will be to reduce the significance of out-of-district and out-of-state tuition, since according to court interpretations, a student's legal residence is the place where he is registered to vote, not the residence of his parents. Colleges that attract students from out-of-district and out-of-state will lose the extra tuition that such students or their districts of residence pay. A Kansas judge has ruled that a junior college cannot charge higher tuition to adult students whose parents live outside the state. If this interpretation of legal residence is not overruled by higher courts, tuition-free or low-tuition colleges may be faced with an influx of students from high-tuition colleges that will parallel the migration of people from states with low welfare payments to those with more generous subsidies.

Ironically, in no state are the financial implications of the amendment so far-reaching as in tuition-free California where out-of-state tuition accounts for $2.2 million for all colleges. Interdistrict attendance agreements alone involve as much as that amount. Under the state subsidy program, California colleges also receive lower payments for "defined adults" (those over twenty-one taking fewer than ten class hours per week) than for regular students. The new ruling renders almost all part-time students defined as adults since the age factor of the definition goes down to eighteen. Estimates of the loss of state payments vary from $10 to $15 million (*Legislative Newsletter,* 1972).

Faced with the threat of similar losses, most states are considering or adopting legislation to redefine residency requirements. Some are attempting to strengthen existing laws; others are accepting the interpretation of Governor Ray of Iowa, who takes the position that "If a person is old enough to vote, he or she is old enough to be vested with other responsibilities, privileges, and obligations of adulthood" (*Higher Education in the States,* 1972, p. 59). Until declared unconstitutional by a June 1973 Supreme Court decision, other states followed a residency policy which made it difficult for an out-of-state student to establish residence for tuition purposes. At the same time the Court ruled that a state may charge higher tuition for non-residents than for residents. In the ruling the Court did not settle the issue of the length of time a student had to reside in a state before acquiring resident status (*Chronicle of Higher Education,* June 18, 1973, p. 1).

If the Supreme Court ruling of March 21, 1972, that thirty days is a sufficient period of time for a state to complete the necessary administrative checks to prevent fraud in voting matters is applied to college attendance, then all nonresidency laws and regulations for tuition purposes may be declared unreasonable. Low-tuition colleges may then have to resort to higher tuition to reduce their attractiveness to students from high-tuition colleges.

A second influence on future tuition patterns (which affects only colleges partially financed through a tax on property) are the court decisions declaring unconstitutional certain aspects of the financing of schools through the property tax. If upheld, these decisions may lead to state financing of community colleges, which, in turn, may lead to more colleges imposing tuition, and higher tuition in colleges where it is already charged. A more tentative, but equally notable prospect is that if one or more of the proposed voucher or loan bank plans should be adopted, tuition will become a certainty in all colleges. Loans, along with scholarships and work-study grants for low-income students, will undoubtedly increase in the near future. At the same time, they will make it easier for colleges to increase tuition on the assumption that the financial aid will take care of most of the students who need it to remain in college, an assumption that is not warranted by the amount of aid presently available.

However, in the Education Amendments of 1972, Congress took a long step in the direction of tuition vouchers by providing for basic educational opportunity grants (BEOG) awarded directly to the students rather than indirectly through the colleges (Public Law 92–318, June 23, 1972, Part D, Subpart I, Sec. 411). For 1973 the amount appropriated for this purpose is so small that only first time freshman students are eligible and the amount for each will average only $250 with a range of $50 to $550 (Los Angeles *Times,* July 20, 1973, Part II, p. 10). Eventually, if Congress appropriates sufficient funds the upper limit will be $1400 per year, not to exceed fifty percent of the cost of instruction. Thus when fully funded the no or low tuition colleges will be encouraged to increase tuition since the BEOG's graduated according to the family or student income will cover most of it. Poor students who will receive the highest awards will not be handicapped by the imposition of or increase in tuition.

From all this one must conclude that even though today tuition and fees probably only contribute about 25 percent to the total operating revenues of community colleges, they will be an important source of revenue for community colleges. Their contribution to operating revenues will probably approach one-third before the end of the decade as more colleges increase tuition and impose higher fees for noninstructional purposes. The resort to fees as a source of funds to build student stores, cafeterias, swimming pools, student centers, and athletic facilities may become the rule rather than the exception. In locally supported colleges tuition and fees will become the second most important source of revenue, below state aid and above the property tax.

Chapter VII

※※※※※※※※※※※※※※※※※※※※※※※※※※※※

Federal Aid

Most educators look toward the federal government for relief from the financial crisis. Their hope that the end of the Vietnam War would produce peace benefits, much of them to education, is proving illusory, but educators still hope that a larger share of operating and capital-outlay funds will come from this source. The questions from them is not should federal aid be provided, but rather how much, in what form, and how soon? Orwig (1971) reflected the certainty of educators on this score, as did proposals and recommendations of the Carnegie Commission on Higher Education and the Task Force on Community and Junior Colleges of the Education Commission of the States.

47

Federal aid comes in a variety of packages—so many in fact, that many colleges have an individual, or staff, whose primary function is to keep track of the kind of aid available, and to prepare requests for funds the colleges are eligible to receive. Workshops are held to advise administrators about available funding programs and the procedures for obtaining funds. Government agencies, educational institutions, private publishers, and the media issue circulars, guidelines, and tips on proposal writing. Educators seeking federal support need these aids in order to find their way through the maze of available programs and agencies distributing the funds.

Congressional and presidential priorities are clearly discernible from the funds appropriated for the community colleges. Until 1973, by far the largest aid was allocated to maintain, extend, and improve vocational education programs; develop new programs (Vocational Education Act 1963); and provide training programs to equip persons for work in needed employment fields (Manpower Development Training Act 1962). This emphasis was consistent with the President's 1972 State of the Union Message which featured a new emphasis on career education; a blend of vocational and academic preparation (*U.S. News and World Report,* Jan. 31, 1972, pp. 60–78). The Education Amendments of 1972 confirmed this priority by large authorizations and the establishment of a Bureau of Occupational and Adult Education in the Office of Education.

Other federal aid was earmarked for construction of facilities, purchase of materials, equipment, supplies, professional development of staff, and program development. Special funds for law enforcement programs were also allotted through the Department of Justice. Occasionally, the government provides additional funds to a special institution such as the Navajo Community College.

Appropriations for student assistance for educational opportunity grants, college work-study programs, and loans approaches $2 billion, but since these do not contribute to operating income they are ordinarily not included in the college budgets. Of course, they are significant to colleges. Without them many students would not be able to attend college.

As a percentage of income, the amount of federal aid allocated to an institution is small. Moreover, much of the aid goes to

number of veterans enrolled. While these provisions tie i
aid to student aid, they are nevertheless a step in the (
institutional aid based on enrollment or number of gradu

As a result of adverse court decisions and pre
educators, the President released impounded impact ai
April 13, 1973 (*New York Times,* April 14, 1973). T
however, can not be considered a permanent policy shi
President believes he has precedent for not spending fu
priated by Congress. He is also determined to keep the bu
a $2.68 billion limit by not spending appropriated funds i

The high hopes that followed the passage of the
Amendments Act in June 1972 evaporated by Deceml
the President disclosed his plans for: dismantling som
decentralizing the Office of Education into regional
pounding or not spending appropriations; special revel
in place of categorical aid; increasing student aid; and
such traditional aid as subsidized construction loans, co
resources, and undergraduate instructional equipment.

No increase in funds is provided in the 1973–1
for programs for the disadvantaged, handicapped, deve
tutions, work-study, and cooperative education. Payment
enrolling veterans that were appropriated for 1972–197
withheld. Neither does the budget include funds for
aid. Revenue sharing for education seems to have beer
for at least a year (*Chronicle of Higher Education,* F(
p. 1).

The differences between the provisions of the Hi;
tion Amendments of 1972 and the President's budget of
is causing confusion among student-aid officers. In estal
basic educational opportunity grants, Congress did not e
older programs. Some interpret the law as requiring ap
for existing state-aid programs before new programs cz
mented (*Chronicle of Higher Education,* Feb. 5, 197
the President's budget the older programs are not fund(

Whatever the outcome of the conflict between t
and Congress over the kind of federal aid, subsidies ar
be an important part of federal aid to education. T
places major emphasis on student aid and revenue s!
Congress favors categorical and student aid. Institut

students and therefore contributes only indirectly, if at all, to income. Whenever matching funds are required for student aid as in work-study proposals, federal aid, in fact, depletes the college income. This is also true whenever the appropriations fail to provide adequate funds for administrative overhead.

Actually, federal aid for operating purposes has varied between 2 and 7 percent of the total budget. The variation has been wider for capital outlay since, once a building program has been completed, the need for funds decreases to zero. This form of aid impounded in 1972–1973 will be eliminated if Congress approves the President's 1973–1974 budget. Spencer (1972) found that fifteen states received $34.6 million or 7.5 percent for operations during 1970–1971. He also found that colleges in nine states received $17.6 million or 14.8 percent of the total income from the federal government for capital outlay.

Table 5 illustrates the variety, sources, amount, and percentage of the total income of funds from the federal government to California colleges. The appearance of secondary school categories in the table is accounted for by the fact that the line between secondary schools and community colleges is still not sharply defined in California and a few other states. Colleges are still eligible for such secondary school funds as impact and vocational education aid.

Prospects for federal aid change so rapidly that it is difficult to make predictions beyond a few months. They were high after the passage of the Education Amendments in June 1972; they reached a low point shortly after the elections when the President began unfolding his New Federalism including revenue sharing for education, impoundment of appropriated funds, and curtailment of many categorical aids. In mid-1973, as a result of the disclosures implicating White House aides in the robbery of the Watergate headquarters of the Democratic party, it looked as if Congress might take a more aggressive attitude toward the President and modify or replace his programs.

One feature of importance to educators in the Education Amendments of 1972 provides for institutional aid or cost of education payments based on the number of students receiving education opportunity grants, work-study payments, or loans. An institution is also entitled to a cost of instruction payment on the basis of the

Table 5.
Federal Income Sources of California J[
1967–1968

Income	All Junior C[Purposes (
Federal Income from Federal Sources	
Maintenance and Operation	$ 2,063,7[
Veterans' Education	65,0[
Economic Opportunity Act	2,317,0[
Elementary and Secondary Education Act	41,4[
Miscellaneous Funds	24,7[
Other	1,907,0[
Total	$ 6,419,0[
Federal Income from State Sources	
National Defense Education Act	$ 835,5[
Manpower Development and Training	5,122,0[
Vocational Education Act	3,853,8[
Economic Opportunity Act	102,3[
Elementary and Secondary Education Act	80,4[
Miscellaneous Funds	1[
Other	154,1[
Total	$ 10,148,0[
Federal Income from County Sources	
Forest Reserve Fund	$ 63,0[
Miscellaneous Funds	1,7[
Other	8[
Total	$ 65,[
Federal Income from Local Sources	
Economic Opportunity Act	$ 85,[
Other	2,[
Total	$ 88,[
Combined State and Federal Income	
Vocational Education Act	$ 3,524,[
Preschool Education Aid	46,[
Other	18,[
Total	$ 3,588,[
Total Federal Income	$ 20,310,[
Total Designated and General Income	$320,582,[

Source: McPherran (1969).

directly provided by Congress; it may be included indirectly in the President's revenue-sharing plan if funds are distributed to colleges. Both the President and Congress favor expanding aid to students attending proprietary schools, a policy that already applies to veterans' education benefits. Proprietary schools were also eligible for manpower development funds. Public school educators seem concerned that this new extension of aid to students in proprietary schools will mean lower funds for them and increased competition for students (Shoemaker, 1973).

Federal aid is still far from becoming a major source of income for the community colleges. If economy is the policy for the next few years, it is even probable that appropriations may decrease substantially rather than increase. Decreases notwithstanding, educators consider federal aid for technical-vocational programs, allied health education, construction of facilities, and general and special student aid important for community colleges. Despite its deficiencies and the charge that it has "induced or seduced every level of government, much of industry and all kinds of private agencies" (Glenny, 1972, p. 16), educators believe federal aid can be the difference between survival and bankruptcy. The financial situation is too critical for them to assume a Don Quixote stance.

Chapter VIII

❀❀❀❀❀❀❀❀❀❀❀❀❀❀❀❀❀❀❀❀❀❀❀❀❀❀❀

Miscellaneous Sources of Income

During the past five years colleges have been directing their attention to private and other sources of revenue. Contributions for equipment, land, and buildings have been a significant source of income; funds for operations, except for a few colleges, have been almost negligible.

Nearly every college with vocational-technical programs receives equipment or money from trade unions, businesses, industries, and trade associations. Sometimes the donation consists of a

53

loan of equipment—new or used—or a sizable price discount on materials purchased. Colleges have received such items as data-processing machines, automobiles, motorcycles, planes, livestock, nursery plants, foundry equipment, and testing machines. The value of such donations can run into hundreds of thousands of dollars a year for colleges with large vocational-technical programs.

Land for a campus is a common form of private gift. Long-view College of the Metropolitan Junior College District in Missouri occupies over 100 acres—a gift of a pioneer family in the area. Crafton Hills College in the San Bernardino (California) District is being built on a 523-acre site donated by a long-time resident. Similar gifts have been received by other colleges. Occasionally, a college receives money for an auditorium, swimming pool, or other special-purpose building. A donor gave Genesee Community College in Michigan a Sears Roebuck department store building valued at $2.5 million (Genesee Community College, 1972).

Under special circumstances a college may attract large donations. For instance, during its first years of operation Navajo Community College on the Navajo reservation received donations amounting to more than $2 million for operating income and construction funds from foundations and private sources. Large grants and gifts have also been given to Corning Community College in New York by a foundation associated with the Corning Glass Company and its executives; and to Kellogg Community College, Michigan, by the Kellogg Foundation.

Before state and federal governments began financing student-aid programs on a large scale, private gifts were the principal source of scholarships and loans. College catalogs list numerous examples of gifts contributed by individuals, service clubs, corporations, foundations, faculty members, and departmental and student-body organizations. In addition to the contributions, sizable bequests from alumni and faculty are becoming more numerous.

The deepening financial crisis is forcing more colleges to seek nongovernmental funds by creating development units or foundations to solicit contributions and to manage funds generated from nongovernmental sources. In some colleges these units also help secure federal grants. As the number of financially successful graduates increases, colleges will receive more gifts and bequests.

Many faculty members are also likely future contributors. The total book value of endowment funds for two-year colleges in 1963–1964 was $14.8 million; for 1966–1967, $21.6 million (Simon and Grant, 1972, p. 104). Gifts, as colleges have learned, sometimes impinge on operating income because they do not often provide for administrative and maintenance expenses, which the college must assume. Donations of large college sites may involve a particularly heavy drain on operating revenues for landscaping, maintenance, and security, not to mention the loss of taxes to the district. Gifts may also be obsolescent or in poor repair. Colleges that plan to engage in fund-raising activities will discover that costs run high if professional help is retained. These remarks are not intended to discourage or disparage gifts as private sources of revenue; they are intended as warnings of some pitfalls that may accompany gifts, whether in money, land, or equipment.

Short-term investments of temporary surplus funds accumulated from operating income, contingency accounts, or bond sales are small, but welcome, income producers. Colleges are now much more conscious than formerly of these income-producing opportunities. At times, investment income may be sizable. For Cuyahoga Community College in Cleveland, Ohio, investment income in a plant fund added almost $112,000 during 1970–1971. Four percent or $887,00 of "current income—institutional and general—" also came from this source (Cuyahoga Community College, 1971). For the Metropolitian Junior College District in Kansas City, Missouri, comparable amounts for the same period were $700,000 for the plant fund and 2.5 percent or $131,000 for the general fund (Metropolitan Junior College District, 1971 pp. 2, 4).

A district building one or more campuses is likely to have large unexpended funds to invest in short-term notes, whereas one without anticipated or planned large expenditures for capital outlay is not likely to have such funds. As surplus funds diminish, as they have for many colleges, investment income must concomitantly diminish.

Investment income from bond funds (arbitrage bond profit) is restricted by the federal Treasury Department to 0.5 percent of the difference between the interest on the bonds and the profit on reinvestment of temporarily unused proceeds from the sale of the bonds. In June 1972 the Treasury Department proposed to reduce the allowable difference to 0.125 percent. The penalty for violating this revision is withdrawal of the tax-exempt status of the bonds.

Investments, notes, and bonds do not represent all the miscellaneous sources of income. Some colleges are selling curriculum materials, but usually at a cost not exceeded by the cost of preparation and reproduction of such material. Other colleges sell films, videotapes, and patented specialized equipment.

Bookstores are profitable enterprises, especially in large colleges, providing profits ranging from $50,000 to $100,000 per year. Parking areas and structures may also generate revenues of comparable proportions. Eating facilities such as dining rooms, cafeterias, and vending machines are less profitable—as often as not a deficit operation.

Profits from the various auxiliary enterprises are sometimes allocated to the associated student body organization and do not contribute directly to college income. The profits help the college indirectly, however, by relieving pressure on the operational funds for subsidizing student activities.

All these sources together still form a small fraction of the income of a public college. Some sources, such as investment income, are temporary; one-time bequests of land help in the formative years of a college. It will be a long time before the income provided approaches a point where a college can depend on any of it continuously, though these sources are potentially attractive. The rising trend of private contributions to public colleges, including community colleges, for the past several years confirms this observation. Private donations to public colleges have risen from 17.8 percent of the total in 1967–1968 to 22 percent in 1970–1971 (*Chronicle of Higher Education*, Jan. 24, 1972, p. 5). How much of this has gone to community colleges is not known—it is probably a small, but growing, percentage.

Chapter IX

❀❀❀❀❀❀❀❀❀❀❀❀❀❀❀❀❀❀❀❀❀❀❀❀❀❀❀

Control of Expenditures

It has been noted that revenues have risen, but not at the rate educators believe necessary—for this the outlook is bleak. Consequently, educators have sought control of expenditures as one of the avenues out of the financial crisis. They "cannot think only in terms of raising more money to solve increasing operations and capital expenditure costs; they must look also to improved methods and techniques to make the most of resources available to them. They must review the programs and activities in terms of cost effectiveness" (Calais, 1972, p. 4). The signposts point to economies of operation, cutbacks in services, reduced enrollment, or a combination of all these.

Changing a course in any institution is a slow, painful process. Eric Walker, former president of Pennsylvania State University, more bluntly stated that "educators rarely ask how much money can be saved and how costs can be lowered—how the system can become more efficient, and how it can deliver more education per dollar spent;" for them "efficiency is a dirty word" (Chapman, 1971). Equally reluctant to change are some instructors who "act as surrogate programmed learning devices" moving "information which could be better moved by film, television, or other devices" (Chapman, 1971, p. 5). Contrary to popular opinion, the heralded participatory democracy, after an initial flurry of activity (sometimes significant as in the introduction of Black Studies), becomes one of the most serious deterrents to change.

This is particularly true of some curriculum committees which, because of their interminable deliberations and procedures, are considered the deathbed of new courses and curriculums. Ideas that might lead to less reliance on the instructor or classroom instruction are particularly vulnerable to rejection. Finally, educational bodies, like all established institutions, have built-in organizational patterns and policies that inhibit change. Except for graduate schools and research centers, they emphasize the status quo. Furthermore, administrators are required to share important financial and educational decision making with representatives of the National Education Association (NEA), American Federation of Teachers (AFT), American Association of University Professors (AAUP), and independent faculty associations. (See Chapter Two for a discussion of collective bargaining.)

The pessimism caused by the resistance to change is somewhat mitigated by the efforts many educators are making to adapt to austerity. Several examples of practices that are enabling colleges to survive are cited by B. L. Johnson (1969); he lists over one hundred colleges in twenty-seven states that are experimenting in as many different directions. However, Johnson does not stress the possible savings of the innovation over the cost of the practice it replaces. Johnson, now Director of the League for Innovation, obtained a grant to study and analyze courses which have been effective in increasing the efficiency of instruction. This study (Berchin, 1972) provides a basis for colleges to increase their efficiency of instruction, keeping in mind both costs and results.

In the college of 1979, Cohen (1969) places reliance on an instructional staff converted "to the idea of specifying learning objectives in precise terms," an innovation that will cost the community college of 1979 "no more to operate than it did in 1969 or even in 1959" (p. 199). He believes that this happy condition will come about because, with behavioral objectives, colleges can be financed "on the basis of student achievement rather than on average daily attendance," full-time student equivalent, or credit hour; it can use differentiated staffing; it can substitute a limited number of core courses for the present profusion of course offerings; and eliminate functions extraneous to the learning process (pp. 40–41). Unfortunately, this is an ideal whose time is further in the future than 1979.

With increasing frequency college administrators are addressing themselves to reform of educational practices and to economies necessary for budget balancing. These examples do not add to a ground swell; they form a slight bulge on the horizon. The failure of the Oakland (Michigan) systems approach to teaching and learning (see Chapter Sixteen), the resistance to large classes, and the slight use of television and other technological devices are reminders that educational changes come very slowly.

Nevertheless, and in spite of their predilections, educators find themselves operating simultaneously on several fronts to resolve their financial problems. Their distaste for cutting back programs, reducing staff, and introducing labor-saving devices and procedures does not mean that they are ignoring such measures. Survival requires that they attend to these areas even while they are pushing for more revenue.

Confrontation with cost cutting may come at any time of the year as a result of a lower-than-expected enrollment, an unexpected veto of an increase in the state appropriation, a mandate for reserving a percentage of state aid, unanticipated higher costs resulting from salary increases required by law, or failure of a tax or bond measure. In meeting these emergency (and long-term) situations, administrators may follow one or more strategies or plans to reduce expenditures by the amount necessary to balance available resources.

Chapter X

※※※※※※※※※※※※※※※※※※※※※※※※※※※※※※

Financial Planning
and Responses

One of the more positive results of the current financial crisis is a reexamination of budget-making procedures. In the long run it may even result in a moderate reform of the educational process.

Educational budget making usually involves a good deal of maintenance of the status quo. A common procedure is to start with the budget of the current year as a basis for developing the next. A supplementary budget incorporates additions required to finance new instructional programs, additions or alterations to the physical facilities or new supporting nonteaching personnel. In the more flush days a third budget supplement incorporated innovative practices that constituted an unusual departure from past practices.

This practice is being changed. More than likely, the basic budget becomes the one in which no net increase is proposed. This version may even involve a decrease in the operating resources since some items such as district retirement contributions, salary increments, pay adjustments of nonteaching personnel to meet salary increases of comparable classifications in the community, insurance, and service on debt obligations constitute fixed or quasi-fixed charges which cannot be easily reduced. The budget may also include either a new freeze on positions or a continuation or modification of one.

New budget procedures, such as simulated budget models, wider participation by the staffs, and the program-planning budget system (PPBS), are gaining favor. A trial run of PPBS by ten California community colleges is in process. For example, San Bernardino College (California) has "programs for each department—student help, supplies, services, repairs, replacement, and new equipment—approximately 60 percent towards complete PPBS" (Jensen, 1972b). Since the system is not easy to implement, progress is slow, but it is expected that this technique may significantly improve management procedures. The St. Louis District is also using simulated budget models for its three colleges. Differences among "the colleges, the need for different resources allocation programs, the different mix of educational programs, size of physical plant, growth and enrollment patterns, student characteristics, faculty rank and load, and class size" are among the variables that must be recognized and that make budget planning such a complicated process (Calais, 1972, p. 11)'.

Administrators are beginning to concentrate on strategies for budget balancing and ways of making budget cutting a more acceptable style of life on campus. Wider participation by faculty and students, more information and discussion, and the greater use of guidelines form important components of budget-making processes today.

Guidelines for the preparation of the budget are not new. In the form of instructions they have nearly always accompanied the annual preparation of the budget. What is new is the added emphasis on establishing parameters for the participants in this annual rite, and the inclusion of more personnel as participants. Formerly the budget was prepared by the budget officer, the president, and a few key administrators. The new approach has additional importance: the necessity for annual budget cutting requires that the process receive more attention from the administrators and more participation by members of the college community. Colleges that are accepting faculty and student participation find that it helps eliminate the attitude "that the planning and management process was . . . just a lot of red tape to keep them from 'doing their thing' . . . that possibly just the opposite was true" (Calais, 1972, p. 10).

It should be noted that faculty and student participation in budget-making is not yet a widespread practice since some trustees and administrators still jealously guard their prerogative in this area. However, faculty, and less often, students participate in the budget-making process in one of four major ways: by working as members of a committee from the beginning to the completion of the budget, when it is presented to the board; by assisting chairmen or unit heads in preparing the departmental or unit budget requests; by taking part in the collective bargaining process; by attending hearings where campus representatives present their criticisms and suggestions for revision of the budget. As collective bargaining spreads, the faculty exerts a major influence on the final budget. The items they are interested in—salaries, fringe benefits, working conditions—comprise about 50 percent of the total expenditures of a college. Nonteaching personnel are also taking a greater interest in this process through their own representatives.

As participation on all levels increases, training in budget making and its significance to the educational process becomes a high-priority item. At professional meetings various aspects of the financial crisis rank among the top two or three topics for panel discussions, seminars, and general sessions; predictably, budgeting gets a large share of attention. Graduate schools of education are revising curriculums to equip their students for the new campus realities. Some districts are even turning to their budget officers when replacing the chief executive.

Most of the guidelines and priorities for budget making which are coming into sharper focus are based on legislation. They are designed to control costs and ensure the proper expenditures of funds. As the financial situation worsens, the number of these laws and regulations increases and those that have been in operation are tightened.

State guidelines and program priorities describe or give clues as to which programs will be funded and which will not. They suggest to administrators which programs and services they must have or support if they hope to receive favorable consideration of their proposals or special grants, and give them high-level support to cut services and programs extended beyond the district's ability to finance them adequately. In attending to the priorities that are not prescriptive, local administrators still have choices to make. For example, they may have to choose whether to fund from their own resources low-priority programs that are inadequately funded by the state. Locally controlled colleges have more options in this regard than state-controlled institutions.

In their local guidelines community college administrators rely heavily on formulas in the allocation of funds. Illustrative is the extensive set of formulas used by the business affairs office of the Chicago City Colleges. Recently revised as a result of a budget deficit, the formulas cover items such as administration, nonacademic positions, adult education, community services, academic salary correction, transfer correction factor, counseling, library, books, travel and telephone, service contract, plant operation, and the disadvantaged (Hill, 1972). Collective bargaining agreements may also contain formulas that must be taken into account by the college administrators in preparing guidelines. They contain minimum and maximum criteria for such factors as salaries, student-teacher ratio, sabbaticals, and work week. Agreements may also cover such items as the number of secretaries and student aides per department, minimum number of instructors required for released time and/or salary increment for department chairmen, and amount of money for convention attendance (McHugh and O'Sullivan, 1971).

Although an explanation of the financial circumstances which make it necessary to reduce expenditures has become an important part of guidelines, in general, directives need not be elaborate. A widely publicized model is that used at Princeton University. Half the guidelines describe financial circumstances which department chairmen, heads of departments, and directors of programs were asked to keep in mind while completing forms for the 1971–1972 operating budget. The other half is taken up with the specific dollar or personnel guidelines (Bowen, 1970).

A review of one community college president's guidelines for budget preparation for 1970–1971, 1971–1972, and 1972–1973 reveals the extent of the financial bind and the progressively more prescriptive measures required. For the 1970–1971 budget, the six guidelines given did not include any which required the maintenance of the status quo or a reduction of expenditures. The only warning was to prepare a detailed explanation of any budgetary item reflecting a significantly larger request than the previous year (Jensen, 1969).

The 1971–1972 guidelines allowed "for *no increases* in supplies and student help" and required *"reductions in all other areas"* (emphasis added). In the guidelines the president explained that the college was operating on a deficit budget and the prognosis for the following years was even worse. A few thoughts were included about "switching to positive thinking" and considering the "problems as really opportunities to show what the college can and will do to continue its excellent instructional program" (Jensen, 1971)'.

The president's prediction for 1972–1973 proved distressingly accurate. In the third series of budget guidelines the prescriptions on cutting were more explicit. Each department was reminded that: it must cooperate in cutting the student help item by 15 percent and the consumable supplies by at least 10 percent; there will be no replacement of equipment unless it is broken; repairs of equipment must be kept to a bare minimum; no purchase of new or additional equipment will be allowed; and no major repair jobs or alterations to buildings or rooms will be made. As a consoling thought, the president ended the memo: "Although we have less time to prepare the budget forms, it should be an easier job, with so little room to maneuver and no room for dreaming" (Jensen, 1972a).

Even with the most carefully planned and executed budgets, unexpected reverses, such as an unanticipated low enrollment, or a governor's veto, may force an administrator to take steps to balance the budget of the college. There are various ways this may be done, depending on the seriousness of the unforeseen circumstances and the exigencies and resources of the particular college.

One of the common reactions to a serious financial difficulty is to place a freeze on positions and plant services. At the beginning of a freeze, all hiring is stopped. Later, modifications may be made to permit replacement of specific vacancies and additions to a department if they do not involve an increase in the total number of employees, or if addition results in a "proven monetary savings to the institution," or "where the change reflects an improved balance of staffing such as lateral transfers" (Macomb County Community College District, 1971, pp. 9–10). Measures prohibiting promotions, eliminating sabbaticals, restricting travel, reducing the number of telephones and long-distance calls, and enjoining purchases of institutional equipment except under special circumstances are generally associated with a freeze. Plant services are curtailed by reducing schedules for repairs, replacement of equipment, cleaning of buildings, and gardening.

An emergency may be incorporated in a budget so that its economies continue into the next fiscal year. More likely, however, a different strategy will be adopted at that time. It may involve an across-the-board percentage cut of money, or personnel, or both. Such action may be made necessary by the legislature, as in 1971 in Michigan, when 2 percent of state aid was ordered held in reserve. Both measures—freezes and across-the-board cuts—have the appearance of fairness and equality of treatment. More important to the administrator, they are easy to implement. However, in practice they are among the worst economy methods, despite their attractiveness to administrators and trustees who do not want to assume the onus of selective cuts. Because they affect all facets of the college operations—good, mediocre, and inferior, with apparent equal impact, they ensure the continuance of marginal divisions, disciplines, courses, services, and personnel. These drain revenues needed to bolster successful activities, introduce new programs and replace old equipment. Plant and equipment deteriorate. Recruiting new employees is slowed down while younger, recently hired employees are terminated. Not only do unit costs rise since the older employees usually make higher salaries, but existing policies become more entrenched, and efficiency suffers since the older employees are less likely to be venturesome or aware of new technologies and processes. In addition, a percentage cut in a small department may be more devastating than the same percentage cut in a large department. A cut of equipment will have far less effect on the English or history departments than on the physics, chemistry, or technical-vocational departments (Brown, 1972, p. 8).

Despite these disadvantages, broad cuts do bring some quick relief. They assure the Board of Trustees and the public that something serious is being done; alert the personnel to the critical nature of the financial situation and the possibility of other economies that may follow; and enable administrators to gain time, either until new money eases the crisis, or until they may create a more rational plan to bring expenditures into line with revenues. They also relieve department or section heads of an unpleasant chore. Since they are so close to their operation, they cannot and probably should not be asked to make the initial emergency cuts in their operations.

A third strategy used in controlling expenditures is to make selective cuts of personnel, equipment, courses, activities, and services. Of these, cuts in personnel and marginal activities are the most difficult to effect. Contracts, tenure, and seniority force administrators to exercise extreme caution in reducing personnel. With the exception of temporary employees, personnel cuts cannot be made until the end of the contractual period and even then must take tenure into consideration. No sooner is a plan to eliminate a department or activity announced than pressure groups are formed to plead with the administration or enlist support of trustees, legislators, and influential citizens for stopping the proposed action.

Some administrators have had success in overcoming this opposition by careful planning and gradual phasing out of a program through normal attrition of personnel or by transfer to other departments or activities. Other administrators have exacerbated their difficulty by not heeding the signs of decline in a department as revealed by enrollment trends. For example, the decline in foreign languages, mathematics, sciences, and engineering has been evident for some time. Administrators have had time to make adjustments in most of these areas. Ups and downs in the popularity of subjects are not new to higher education, neither among the liberal arts nor among technical-vocational areas. They are easily spotted if a careful semester-by-semester record is kept of enrollments in the courses. Unfortunately, too many colleges have been accustomed to rising overall enrollments which tend to offset the effects of weaknesses in particular subject areas. At such times the overall unit cost either decreases or remains constant. In a period of depression, however, there are few, if any, prosperous departments that can make up for the excessively high unit cost of depressed departments.

In addition to providing a gauge with which to test the viability of courses and programs, selective cutting gives educators the opportunity to reexamine the principle that a community college has an obligation to be the dispenser of every service that can be labeled community. They can consider offering only those commensurate with the resources the community is willing to allocate. This will require careful choosing and setting of priorities. It may lead to the elimination of unnecessary or minimally useful services and those that duplicate services of other agencies.

Auxiliary services, not directly related to the instructional program or offered to adults, are receiving close scrutiny by state legislatures and state boards. Such activities as day-care centers, little theaters, lecture series, dancing classes, and recreational and noncredit classes are either being prohibited, classified as nonreimbursable programs, or required to be self-supporting. Many colleges that continue to offer these services keep costs under control by requiring a fee, especially for noncredit courses, lectures, concerts, and other activities. Even though the fees may not cover the full cost, they do reduce the drain on finances.

Probably the most popular cost-cutting strategy is the reduction of administrators. These cuts have great appeal to board members, faculty, and the public. The high salaries of administrators, the large size of their staffs, and perquisites such as well-furnished offices, automobiles, membership in civic clubs, and expense accounts, make them popular targets for the economy-minded. In this category, across-the-board cuts are easier to effect since administrators do not have the support of powerful organizations and find it difficult to justify their salaries, perquisites, and staff.

One of the more spectacular examples of administrative cuts was taken by the Seattle Community College Board of Trustees.

Instead of replacing the chancellor, the Board created a council of three presidents to coordinate the activities of the college and conduct the business of the district. Each president serves as chairman for one year. By this administrative restructuring the district expects to affect a savings of $100,000 during 1973–1975 (*Chronicle of Higher Education,* Dec. 4, 1972, p. 4).

Among other administrative cuts, boards of trustees are also scrutinizing institutional memberships, dropping those that are not related to the goals and purposes of the college or are not performing their mission. As with other budgetary items the number of these organizations has multiplied. One Middle West multicampus district listed twenty-five institutional memberships, most of which require annual membership fees. But dues are only part of the cost of membership; larger than the dues are the expenses of attendance at meetings and conferences. Trustees, instructors, and students were encouraged to attend such gatherings. Other measures include restricting the number of persons who may attend the same conference within the state; prohibiting or limiting attendance at out-of-state meetings to one person; limiting the number of times within the year an individual may attend a conference; and placing a limit on the amount of money allotted to a person for attendance at a conference. In a few instances, boards or state agencies have so severely cut funds for this purpose as to make such attendance impossible (Hartford, 1971, p. 39). Though not significant in the amount saved, these cuts are symptomatic of the scrutiny trustees and administrators are giving to all budget items.

Concern about the growth of staffs and functions of professional associations has also arisen. Association directors, like administrators of colleges, react to a problem and an opportunity for service by increasing "the central staff and attempting to solve the problem or provide the service from the central staff," rather than making use of short-term groups. This leads to increased dues. The Santa Barbara Community College Board by resolution asked the California Junior College Asssociation to ensure that dues are equitably assessed and that the association effect economies of operation just as member districts are doing (California Junior College Association, February 1972, p. 3).

Though administrative cuts produce a relatively small saving (administrative expenses account for about 20 percent of the total budget), administrators and trustees find it necessary to make more than a gesture in this vulnerable area. When they do not, economies in the instructional division meet stiffer faculty and board opposition. In practice, therefore, this area must receive attention early in order to take some of the sting away from cuts affecting faculty and other personnel. Besides their popularity and favorable effect, administrative cuts provide opportunities for review of the administrative structure leading to reforms that may improve efficiency and act as a brake on the trend toward multiplication of administrators.

These remarks are not intended to imply that the faculty, mollified by administrative cuts, remain uncritical. Often, measures that are taken in that area give them the opportunity to call for more. Local 1600 AFT-CIO of the Chicago Colleges countered the Chancellor's proposals for meeting a $3.9 million deficit in 1971–1972 with one of its own calling for even more drastic cuts in the Chancellor's office and fewer (if any) affecting chairmen and faculty. Faculty representatives at Macomb County Community College, in a similar move, recommended that the central administration be kept to a maximum of 4 percent of the total operating budget, thereby saving $1 million (Macomb County Community College District, minutes, special meeting of board of trustees, Feb. 15, 1972).

Chapter XI

❀❀❀❀❀❀❀❀❀❀❀❀❀❀❀❀❀❀❀❀❀❀❀❀❀❀

Improving Managerial Efficiency

One overriding aspect of the financial crisis in the community college enterprise relates to managerial efficiency. The area has received some attention but not as much as it has in other enterprises, perhaps because the phenomenal growth of the colleges overshadowed all other considerations, and because the personal consequences of a financial crisis are not as serious for educational managers as they are for managers in business. The general attention in education focuses on lack of funds as the major cause of the financial crisis—

as is true of any financial crisis. In education, however, the general assumption is that the enterprise is soundly managed and will continue to function effectively if enough funds are appropriated; only rarely are the managers called to account for the financial deterioration of their institution.

Moreover, the educator has less freedom in his management of finances than his business counterparts. State laws restrict him in many ways. Methods of accounting are so closely regulated that it is difficult to make judgments on efficiency as long as the educational manager has followed the rules. One might even state that an administrator would hesitate to introduce a more efficient method of using resources if the new method involved a serious deviation from the regulations. Also, managerial effectiveness in education, closely linked and similar to teaching effectiveness, has eluded measurement.

In one sense, the very regulations that are designed to protect the public's money from misuse can lead to higher costs. The purposes and sometimes the amount of funds that may be used are often prescribed. Accounting procedures are constrictive. Line item budgeting makes it difficult to transfer funds from one line or account to another. Budgeting practices place a premium on spending all yearly appropriations. A frugal administrator who reports a surplus at the end of the year will be rewarded by a reduced budget the following year. In some states, once an activity has been established in a college it becomes illegal to substitute a non-college-operated activity such as a leasing arrangement with a food service. For example, if the Los Angeles Community College District should find that a private contractor could offer the same or better food service at a lower cost than that provided by its own operation, it could not make the change since this would be construed as an attempt to circumvent the merit system for cafeteria employees who would be displaced by the change. This is an extreme case, but others of a similar nature could be cited.

The nature of education has eluded measurement, and educators have resisted attempts to apply statistical measures for determining success, educationally or financially. They maintain that comparisons with profit-making enterprises are fallacious; that their operations are more closely analogous to publicly owned enterprises like the Post Office and transit systems which are required to perform services that must be subsidized to make up the difference between their cost and the fees charged. Community college educators required to maintain an open-door or open-access policy by a legislature have even less control over much of the costs of operation.

Practical and theoretical consideration aside, concern for the effective expenditures of the large amounts allocated to education has raised questions about the managerial qualifications of educational administrators. Their alleged inexperience in management and their inability to use effectively personnel and material resources are considered major shortcomings. Auditors and legislative committees have been critical of specific examples of poor budget management, faulty enrollment projection techniques, low class sizes, inadequate scheduling of classrooms and other space, and unwise purchase of expensive equipment. One state auditor claimed he found a million dollars worth of discarded carrels, programmed materials, and other equipment at a college. Some critics maintain that during the tremendous rise in enrollment educators should have done better than just maintain per capita cost on a level with the declining value of the dollar. With enrollments doubling every three or four years they should have taken the opportunity to effect reforms in the technology of teaching that could have reduced per capita cost and eased the pressure on taxes. These examples plus the publicized incidents of alleged failures in administering financial aid indicate that more attention is needed to train educators in financial management, particularly since so many managers (administrators) are selected from the ranks of inexperienced instructors. Spurred by the financial crisis and estimates that expenditures can be decreased by 10–20 percent, a change is taking place. Community college educators are looking to management reforms, many of which are adapted from business practices; so far the reforms are being introduced piecemeal. Nevertheless, some educators are remedying deficiencies through improved management techniques in budget making or deployment of faculty through new technologies of instruction and improved use of physical facilities. These new techniques do not add up to scientific management system, but they do point to the educators' awareness and application of management principles in the operation of the college.

No attempt will be made to describe the many current and past theories of organization and management being urged upon educators. A continuum of managerial efficiency exists under any theory. An administrator must choose the system suited to himself, modified by the situation in the college and the individuals with whom he must operate. The 1972 law-and-order environment is different from that of 1964–1969. Yet, an administrator who tries to govern today as many of his pre-1964 predecessors did will find himself in difficulty despite law-and-order-oriented boards of trustees. Moreover, even if the claims for the latest theory—participation, group involvement, human development—are incontrovertible, many do not have the option "to wait as long as three years to see any significant change in end-result variables, and to wait as long as ten years to see a maximization of such results" (Richardson, Blocker, and Bender, 1972, p. 107). Most of them will not be in office in ten years, many not even in three.

President Charles E. Rollins (1972) of Bucks County Community College, Pennsylvania, counsels that educators "should be extremely leary of proponents of revolutionary schemes which will solve all of our fiscal problems." Such schemes often prove illusory, "do not work as efficiently as their proponents claim," and may even exacerbate the financial situation. Rather, he insists that hard work and hard decisions "are required with [presidential] leadership and coordination in fiscal planning as a continuous, sequential process . . . adaptable to changes in allowing for updating."

Whether or not a college should lease data-processing equipment to create a data base for a management information system or add an institutional research officer to the staff depends on the size of the college, its resources, and the services that will be performed that are not or cannot be performed by regular staff. Even the program planning budget system (PPBS) may be an expensive innovation when costs are compared with savings. Of 505 colleges responding to a questionnaire, 22 percent reported they had an institutional research office, 31 percent that they were using PPBS, and 15 percent that they employed management information service techniques. Only a small percentage replied that they had all three (Bogard, 1972). Before the advent of the computer, colleges were able to (and many still do) gather extensive information from their various administrative divisions. Efficiently operated offices have detailed information on their current and past operations to enable the president, as well as other administrators, to evaluate whatever aspect of the college operations he wishes, determine what is happening, compare it with the past, and make judgments on the immediate future. If a president has an institutional information or research officer, he can obtain more sophisticated, statistical analyses and conclusions based on this information. As important as machines and systems for decision making, is the attitude of the president, other administrators, and faculty to this information. Studies abound, but their use has not matched their quantity.

It may be too much to expect a discontinuance of the practice of placing inexperienced instructors in management positions from department chairmen to president, but it is reassuring that the importance of training in management is being recognized. In-service training programs for administrators are becoming as common as those for instructional staff. Federal funds and foundation grants supplement college appropriations for these purposes. These leadership and training programs include units on "labor relations, squeezing unit costs, efficient production, meeting impossible budgets" (Tickton, 1971, p. 13), aspects presidents rank highest as sources of pressure. With this kind of assistance, educators may be in a better position to assure the best use of funds.

Particular attention is being directed toward strengthening the business and financial units of the administrative organization. The business manager is likely to be a coordinate officer with other second-echelon administrators and with the academic title dean or vice-president. Resistance of the academic staff toward him as an academic officer is still strong but not quite as strong as a few decades ago. His stature has grown as colleges have grown in size and complexity, requiring his expert management of finances. Business officers in their turn are giving more attention to the educational nature of the enterprise. Boards are beginning to lean toward business managers as successors to their present chief executives.

Managerial efficiency cannot be reduced to a formula

acquired in a university program or from a theorist and successfully applied to solve financial difficulties on a college campus. When colleges were small, faculties submissive, and budgets modest, management and budget balancing were relatively easy tasks. During the 1930s colleges suffered from the effect of the Great Depression but administrators had freedom to make adjustments. For example, salary cuts encountered little faculty opposition; furloughs or unpaid holidays during the Easter and Christmas holiday periods were a common practice for reducing expenses; workloads were increased at will with little organized remonstrance from the faculty.

Today, colleges are large, with financial commitments running into millions of dollars, with well-organized faculty and non-teaching personnel, and with complex administrative structures—all of which deprive presidents of the easy options of their predecessors.

At the same time, the president's authority has been circumscribed by a multiplication of state agencies created by legislatures to supervise or coordinate the activities of the various segments of higher education. Glenny (1972) feels that as a result of this and other developments, "the ostensible leaders of institutions of higher education, that is, their presidents and governing boards, are the leaders of the institutions mainly in title and visibility" (pp. 21–22).

Whether or not one agrees with Glenny's dour observation, it lends weight to the need for more training in the managerial and financial aspects of education. Administrators may take some comfort in the realization that the adjustments they have to make are not very different from those business managers have made to restrictive legislation and strong unions.

The attention given to more efficient management practices may enable community college educators to help forestall early closing of schools, bankruptcy, or discontinuance of operation. To maintain this minimum survival level will require great managerial ability in the next five years if predictions of tighter budgets, increased inflation, and lower enrollments should materialize.

Chapter XII

✿✿✿✿✿✿✿✿✿✿✿✿✿✿✿✿✿✿✿✿✿✿✿✿✿✿✿✿✿✿

Per Capita Costs

Without knowledge of costs, not much sense can be made out of a possible resolution of the financial crisis. In this discussion, emphasis will be on the unit or per capita cost as the figure that stands out most prominently in a cost analysis.

Per capita cost is generally derived by dividing the total cost of operation by the number of full-time equivalent students. Less frequently, it is determined by cost per credit hour—total cost divided by the number of credit hours taken by students. Per capita cost nearly always refers to current expense of education; rarely to capital-outlay expenditures, which are kept in a separate category.

Sometimes excluded in determining per capita cost are expenditures for community services, adult education, and student activities, since these are considered auxiliary services peripherally related to the regular program of instruction and are often partially or wholly self-supporting. Also commonly excluded are state and federal funds for student financial aid. The total cost of education is always higher than the current expense of instruction by a margin of approximately 10 percent.

Per capita cost has as much significance to educators, governors, legislators, and trustees as net earning per share has for their counterparts in business. However, whereas businessmen look for a larger annual net earnings per share, educators hope for a stable or at most a small rise in per capita cost of instruction every year. Businessmen have a greater incentive for reversing a downward curve of net earnings than educators have in changing the direction of an upward curve of per capita cost. They are expected to show a profit.

A rising curve of per capita cost is not necessarily a cause for alarm among educators. They often interpret it as a favorable statistic, an index of the commitment of a community to support education and proof of the high quality of education. Colleges are often rated on the amount they spend—the higher the amount, the higher the rating (O'Neill, 1971, pp. 43–45).

Questions, however, have been raised about the adequacy and interpretation of per capita cost of instruction. "Discussions of change in the cost of education would make much better sense," according to Machlup (1970), "if the products of education were measurable, say, in bits of information received, amounts of knowledge absorbed, or potential intellectual and moral energy stored up" (p. 83). This, he adds, is not possible. All that can be done is to measure the inputs (dollars) required to supply educational services to a certain number of students for a certain number of hours per year. Machlup also differentiates between the required cost of a given task and the increase in the demand for education caused by more people in a particular age group going to college or staying in college for a longer period of time.

Toombs maintains that the per capita cost concept, derived

from business practices, while useful and worthwhile in demonstrating comparative costs of different methods of instruction, fails to give a clue as to which method or combination gives the best outputs. He insists that instead of concentrating on the labor-intensive characteristic of education, educators and others should consider education as quality intensive (1972, pp. 24, 29).

A research group sponsored by the Western Interstate Commission for Higher Education (WICHE) has also found that measuring the products of education is difficult, especially since the staff could not agree "on what higher education actually produces." So far, their most useful indicators are those used by practitioners: class size, student-faculty ratio, and the mix of courses in the curriculum. They hope eventually, however, to apply a systems analysis approach to their studies (*Change,* 1971).

Comparisons of cost must be made with caution because of the large number of variants that enter into its computation. This observation applies to comparisons within a state as well as to those among states; however, comparisons among colleges in different states require the greatest caution. Aside from variations in economic resources and in cost of living among the states, the unit of measurement on which per capita cost is based also varies (see Chapter Four).

The cost per student will vary depending upon the mix of programs that a college offers. A college with a large evening or adult education program, staffed by part-time instructors, has a lower per capita cost than a college with a small program. A three-hour evening class taught by an instructor paid on an hourly basis usually costs from one-half to four-fifths the cost of a similar day class taught by a full-time instructor on a yearly salary.

Courses and programs in the technical-vocational area and those for minority and disadvantaged students increase per capita cost; liberal arts courses and programs have the opposite effect. To illustrate, Wattenbarger found that "Cost differentials as a ratio of [the unit cost of each of] fifty-six programs to the unit cost of liberal arts, general curriculum during 1968–1969 in fifteen colleges" varied from 0.91 for general business to 3.13 for sheet-metal workers (1970, pp. 93–96). Cost differences also exist within each group. Within limits, costs fluctuate directly with the number of curricular programs and courses and inversely with the number of students in any program (Witmer, 1972, p. 111).

Finally, another large determinant of per capita cost revolves around instructors. A high percentage of instructors with long periods of service increases cost since these instructors usually have higher salaries than those with shorter tenure. However, of all the inputs, the weekly teaching load has more effect on per capita cost than any other single factor. A high weekly teaching load can even offset high salaries (Witmer, 1972, p. 111).

As a result of these factors and others, studies of per capita cost show wide differences among states and within a state. A study of twenty-five states in 1969–1970 showed a range of per capita costs for all programs of $437–$2924. States with maximum costs had a range of $1121–$2924 while in states with minimum costs the range was $437–$850. In every comparison, vocational-technical programs had higher per capita cost than parallel university programs. For the former, the low was $770 and the high $5900, while for the latter the range was $549–$2569 (Arkansas, Commission on Coordination of Higher Education Finance, 1970). For individual states, cost differentials usually show narrower differences. For example, in Oregon the operating costs for reimbursable programs varied among the thirteen colleges from $804 to $1471 per FTE for a state average of $1087, while the range among sixty-eight California districts was $644 to $1668 per ADA for a state average of $868. For the forty-six Illinois colleges the range was $1075 to $2798 per FTE for a state average of $1465. In Georgia the range was $1250–$1951 (excluding one college with a cost of $3019) for a state median of $1710.

Administrators have in per capita cost an index that enables them to judge the adequacy with which they are spending public funds. With today's emphasis on fiscal accountability and concern about fiscal management, per capita cost—despite the qualifications surrounding its meaning—should be watched closely. Until a standard for judging quality of educational output has been developed, one must consider the size of per capita cost as a standard by which to judge administrative management of funds. While it is difficult and questionable to draw conclusions on fiscal management solely from this source, educators cannot overlook the implications of this index at any time and especially during a period of financial stringency. The wide differences between districts within a state or within a multicampus district should be analyzed carefully by administrators. Where costs are consistently higher than average, administrators have a responsibility to justify the difference on the basis of quality or special circumstance (high-cost programs, large numbers of minorities, greater mix of programs, better service to students). Otherwise, the criticism that educators spend all they can get will be difficult to refute.

Chapter XIII

❀❀❀❀❀❀❀❀❀❀❀❀❀❀❀❀❀❀❀❀❀❀❀❀❀❀❀❀❀❀

Effective Utilization of Physical Facilities

A possible source of conserving financial resources is the better utilization of physical facilities. Purchase of a site and construction of the physical plant are the most expensive outlays in establishing a new college; both may involve several hundred thousand to several million dollars depending upon the projected student body enrollment. Later, plant operation and maintenance will represent about 11 percent of an operating budget. The average for the eighteen Virginia colleges in 1970–1971 was slightly less than

82

10 percent (*Financing Virginia's College* p. 48), not far from the 11 percent average for the larger Illinois and California systems (Illinois Junior College Board, 1971a, p. 54; Coast Community College District, 1971). Economies in plant operation and management will be small in contrast to those possible in capital outlay. However, effective space planning and utilization can enable the college to reduce capital outlay by reducing the amount of floorspace needed, in addition to the savings made possible by operation and management of a smaller plant.

Interest in better planning and more effective utilization of space, experimentation with new teaching technologies, and the campus building boom were almost contemporaneous events. During the peak of the boom, the Educational Facilities Laboratories (EFL) was funded by the Ford Foundation to make available the latest research on college construction. At the same time, independently and in concert with the EFL, architects, architectural firms, graduate schools of education, and state agencies also offered their services. Through research and experimentation, emphasis in building shifted from fixed and single-purpose spaces to flexible and multipurpose spaces (Educational Facilities Laboratories, 1964). The new ideas on space were disseminated through numerous publications replete with drawings and specifications on buildings, classrooms, auditoriums, laboratories, and other areas. Implied in space utilization is a time dimension, that is, the number of hours per day, days per week, and months per year that space is used.

Five aspects of space and its utilization can result in lower expenditures without adversely affecting the quality of the educational program: construction of flexible and multiple-use rooms and spaces; mix of permanent and temporary facilities; use of community facilities; around-the-clock and year-round use of the plant; and effective utilization of classrooms.

Savings can be made in capital expenditures by flexible arrangements of space and provisions for multiple use of laboratories, auditoriums, physical education areas, and office space. Considerable progress has been made in designing laboratories so they can be used for several disciplines. Large areas are being built so they can be converted into smaller spaces by soundproof partitions. Office space is often reduced by combining reception rooms for two or more administrators and by centralizing clerical personnel and re-production equipment used by faculty and college staff. Large colleges obviate the need for costly additions to cafeteria facilities by using smaller spaces at various spots on campus for automatic vending machines, lunch carts, and even snack bungalows. Econo-mies of a similar nature can be made for study areas and other services.

When building a new campus or adding to an existing campus, administrators are using a mix of moveable or temporary structures and permanent buildings as a means of providing flexi-bility in classroom, office, and other space requirements. Moveable, temporary units cost less than permanent buildings and they are readily disposable if contraction becomes necessary. Some multi-college districts maintain a ratio of 80 percent in permanent struc-tures and 20 percent in temporaries for each college. College populations are not static either in number or in location. The temporary facilities now available are self-contained units with all the conveniences associated with permanent structures. Some new colleges have begun operation in these easily assembled facilities, and established colleges are using them frequently when more space is required.

Savings can also be made in the startup costs of new colleges and capital-outlay expenditures of existing colleges by using com-munity buildings either on a rental or rent-free basis. A large number of colleges start operating in such facilities on a temporary basis and even after a building program has been completed, continue to use them for special programs.

Some educators believe that those who profit from off-campus, work-study, or cooperative education programs should contribute to their cost. In classes close to the students' place of work, such as those in downtown branches of campuses, cooperating employers often provide classrooms. A large program of this kind is conducted by East Los Angeles College in the Los Angeles Civic Center area using rent-free facilities in government office buildings. Lorain County Community College (Ohio) offers special classes for local companies at their plants and at their expense. The great majority of colleges offering nursing, radiological technology, and other paramedical programs are using, without cost, hospital clinical facilities.

Examples of the ultimate use of off-campus facilities are Whatcom Community College in Washington and the Community College of Vermont; they are conducting all operations in public school buildings, stores, and other premises rather than in traditional college buildings (Hamill, 1922; Vermont Regional Community College System, Inc., 1972). In addition to low startup and negligible shutdown costs, the overall operating costs of Whatcom Community College and Community College of Vermont are lower than comparable costs on traditional campuses. The Whatcom and Vermont experiments are similar to a proposal by a former community college educator, John McDaniel, for a Sidewalk Career College (1968, p. 100).

Year-round use of plants, Saturday and Sunday classes, and around-the-clock scheduling of classes effect further capital savings. These continue to have such modest appeal that they are not likely to contribute greatly to the resolution of the financial crisis. The quarter system, a version of year-round scheduling, has been adopted by a considerable number of colleges—probably more for educational than for economic considerations. The evidence on relative cost between the semester and the quarter system is inconclusive. A comparison of operating costs on the quarter and the semester systems in Illinois districts show only a small difference, $49 per credit hour for the former and $48 for the latter (Illinois Junior College Board, 1971a, p. 63).

From the standpoint of efficiency, planning and scheduling of classroom space presently ranks high as an example of poor educational management. A common practice in many community colleges is a high utilization of space during the morning hours which drops markedly in the afternoon; from 2 P.M. to 4 P.M. use of available classrooms rarely exceeds 30 percent.

Criticisms of scheduling a majority of morning classes date back to post-World War II, when the pressure of veteran enrollment taxed classroom capacity during the morning hours. Large enrollments made it necessary to reexamine existing practices and devise new patterns of scheduling. The establishment of new colleges, and huge building programs with the resultant surplus of space, let colleges return to the traditional pattern of high morning and low afternoon utilization (Lombardi and Trigg, 1951).

A Michigan president reported to his faculty that classrooms were used at 61 percent of capacity during morning hours and at 28 percent during the afternoon hours. Usage of the labs and library was comparable in this all too common situation. He added that statistics "show dramatically to the layman that we have space to spare, and he'll never be convinced that before we can fill it, we'll need four thousand more students and a hundred more faculty members" (Greene, 1971, p. 5). Even more embarassing is an official college report that "at least fifty-two [classrooms] are vacant at all times during the day" and that overall average classroom usage of 146 rooms based on a 44-hour week is 50 percent (Lehto, 1972, p. 31).

Criticisms of alleged inefficient classroom utilization and lack of building funds has led to a revival of interest in scheduling patterns that distribute class offerings over a 6–8 hour daily span. Where colleges attempt to establish standards of usage, one of two measures is commonly used: the percentage of student stations (seats), or the percentage of teaching stations (rooms) available during a 30- or 40-hour week. Another measure of utilization, the percentage of student stations used when the rooms are actually occupied, offers little help for determining whether or not the college has adequate, too little, or too much space. Other measures based on square feet of floor space may be used, but these are used more as standards when building classroom structures than in space-utilization studies (Russell and Doi, 1957, p. 17).

The most common measure is room utilization. Since classrooms comprise the major portion of usable space in a college plant, improved planning could result in large savings in capital-outlay funds for new buildings (and even new campuses) and ensure lower maintenance costs. Simply restricting the number of teaching stations would force administrators, faculty, and students to use the facilities at full capacity from morning until late afternoon. With a student population spread over 6 or 8 hours per day instead of 4 hours in the morning, the need for library, lounge, eating, and other auxiliary facilities would also be reduced. In practice this measure requires that usage standards for general classrooms be higher than those for special-purpose rooms such as laboratories and large lecture halls. Utilization of 75 percent for general classrooms and 50 percent of special-purpose rooms, based on a 40-hour week, is reasonable.

This standard is not often achieved. Except in special situations, such as existed after World War II or during a period of unusually high enrollment, utilization is closer to 60 percent for general classrooms and 45 percent for special-purpose rooms. One such study of twenty-six junior colleges indicated the median usage to be 57 percent for general classrooms and 46 percent for laboratories (Doi and Scott, 1960, p. 13).

Since building is likely to be kept in check by the scarcity of funds, colleges are seeking more effective methods of class scheduling, requiring new patterns of working hours for faculty and new attendance patterns for students—the two groups most affected. Usually there is some initial resistance to the changes, but, faculty and students can easily adjust to the revised scheduling and may even find reasons for preferring it since it offers wider choices of working hours and attendance patterns.

More effective utilization of campus classrooms is being achieved by five more or less discrete patterns. A method for laboratory courses is to have two sets of programs, one with morning lecture and afternoon laboratory sections and another with morning laboratory and afternoon lecture sections. This works best with elementary courses that have large enrollments and multiple sections. In advanced courses or those with only one section, intra- and interdepartmental cooperation is necessary to achieve a balanced distribution of classes between morning and afternoon hours. Another procedure is to require each department or group of departments to offer a specified number or percentage of classes during the morning and afternoon hours. A third method is to assign a department or groups of departments a certain number of classrooms based on the average number of sections scheduled during a given period—usually four semesters or six quarters—and on the observable enrollment trends for the courses offered.

Block scheduling of instructors or students are other methods gaining favor. In the former, introduced widely during the mid-

1940s, five or six interlocking schedules, each spanning a 4- or 5-hour period, are prepared. Each instructor, usually on the basis of seniority, selects the schedule he likes. This system works best in academic departments with a large number of instructors.

In the second version of block scheduling, a student is required to choose a morning or afternoon schedule on a first-come, first-served basis, sometimes modified to include class standing according to number of units completed. Class hours are divided into three groups: 7 A.M., 8 A.M., 9 A.M.; 10 A.M., 11 A.M., 12 P.M.; and 1 P.M., 2 P.M., 3 P.M. The middle group is reserved for courses which have only one section, and either morning or afternoon students may choose a class from it. A morning student, however, may not take a class in the afternoon group and vice-versa.

A modification of this is the "Double Schedule" of Cabrillo College (California) "which concentrates a full selection in the morning from 7 A.M. to 12 noon and another selection in the afternoon from 1 P.M. to 6 P.M. . . . Students may enroll in any class listed in any one schedule but may not combine class selections from both schedules." Crossover classes, those with one section, are listed in both schedules (Cabrillo College, 1972, p. 9). In the fall of 1971, the ratio of enrollments was approximately 60 percent morning, 40 percent afternoon, or 2700 morning students to 1500 afternoon students. Two conditions considered necessary for the success of this plan are that there be not more than 30–40 percent of crossover classes and a minimum college enrollment of 4000 (Younger, 1972).

All the methods just described have as their common objective the distribution of classes over the full day the college is in session. They are most effective in reducing expenditures in colleges with limited facilities. Colleges with excess facilities will make little if any saving by redistributing classes throughout the day unless the redistribution results in unused space that can be sealed off. If these areas are then rented, the colleges gain some income; if renting is not feasible, maintenance expenditures are at least reduced. If the excess facilities consist of temporary buildings, the colleges may be able to sell them.

Effective utilization depends on the administrator developing the principle that classrooms, laboratories, auditoriums, and other facilities belong to the college, not to a department or an individual; and that no facility should remain unused when the college needs it. To maintain such a principle requires vigilance to prevent a facility from becoming the domain of any individual or group. Where a special condition prevails that requires an exception to this principle, it should be made only after careful examination of the reasons for the exception.

Classroom utilization studies can and should be made each semester without an excessive amount of effort, time, and personnel. A utilization study of all facilities is a more complicated undertaking that requires greater detail as to location, area, and usage. Such a study, in reality an inventory, may reveal areas not utilized or areas that can be given over to other uses. A periodic, updated inventory of facilities becomes a useful tool when determining space needs of new programs or expansion of existing programs. With this information administrators can develop norms or compare the allocation of space with that of other colleges or with state standards.

Chapter XIV

�✺des✺des✺des✺des✺des✺des✺des✺des✺des✺des✺des✺des✺des✺des

Controlling Low-Enrollment Classes

Despite warnings by consultants and accreditation teams, controlling low-enrollment classes has made uneven progress. In fact, except in a few large-class-size experiments in community colleges the trend has been toward smaller class sizes.

The financial drain created by low-enrollment classes will continue as long as traditional teaching methods remain unchanged and program comprehensiveness is given high priority. When enrollments are increasing, the percentage of small classes is likely, though not certain, to remain within reason. When enrollments are static or decreasing, the percentage rises. Moreover, during a period of expansion, the high costs of small classes are counterbalanced and hidden by the low costs of large classes in the popular or required courses.

Adding courses to the curriculum is an easier process than eliminating those that are marginal in terms of enrollment or unnecessary. Even though colleges attempt to control the number of courses by periodic deletions, courses once added tend to remain in the catalog, regardless of when they were offered last. One reason for retaining them is the belief of department chairmen and faculty members that a large offering of courses adds prestige to their departments. If this were the only effect, their retention in the catalog would not be costly. However, their inclusion creates the temptation to offer one or more of them periodically. Occasionally, a minimum enrollment is obtained, which means a high per student cost and more importantly, added pressure to offer the course again.

At the same time, cuts in courses and programs are often not made in the hope that the enrollment downturn is temporary and will be reversed. Sometimes, since the instructor involved is tenured and not easily displaced, marginal, low-enrollment courses may continue to be offered because it is better to have the instructor teach small classes than no classes. Administrators often acquiesce to small classes because of their desire or the necessity not to discourage experimentation.

Colleges making serious attempts to control the number of low-enrollment classes are proceeding in a variety of ways. The most effective course of action is to control the introduction of new courses. This may be done by requiring the department that requests the addition of a new course to delete an existing course that has not been offered for one or two years. For existing courses, a common practice is to require each chairman, when presenting copy for the new catalog, to justify the inclusion of any course that has not been offered during that year or has been offered but has had a continuous record of low enrollment. In some states the governing boards for the community colleges act as a restraining influence by not approving or funding programs that appear to duplicate those in neighboring colleges.

A campus curriculum committee is a further effective restraint on the addition of courses. Merely by referring a proposal for a course to the committee delays action and also forces the examination of the need for the course. Curriculum committees tend to be conservative in approving new courses (Hefferlin, 1971, p. 5).

A simple, easily monitored expedient for controlling class size is to establish a minimum. The minimum may be ten or fifteen at the close of registration or one week after it closes.

In cases where low-enrollment courses are required for a program or graduation, several procedures might be followed. One is to offer essential courses in alternate semesters or years. For colleges in isolated areas this is the most feasible alternative available. Usually, first-semester courses with low demand are offered only in the fall when the bulk of first-time freshman enroll. Fewer first-semester courses and more advanced courses are offered in the spring semester when the college enrolls a large number of continuing students.

One innovation to curtail the numbers of low-enrollment courses is the cluster concept. Colleges within commuting distance of each other are taking the lead in reducing the number of technical-vocational courses by adopting this system. Clusters concentrate broad programs such as health, in one college, technical, in another, and public service in a third. But clustering is not limited to technical-vocational programs. The Chicago college system, for instance, is considering a plan of concentrating advanced foreign language classes on a few centrally located campuses. With a computerized enrollment system, this offers little difficulty. A student may enroll for any course at any of the cooperating campuses from his resident campus. Another aspect of clustering is to have two or more nearby colleges agree to alternately offer their advanced (and other low-enrollment) courses in mathematics, physics, chemistry, and foreign languages. A student who cannot wait for an advanced course to be offered at his resident college is permitted to take the course at a cooperating college.

Another method of reducing small classes is to schedule two or more classes in the same room with the same instructor. This plan is used effectively in laboratory courses. Similar arrangements are found in foreign language and secretarial laboratories where students may plug into one of a number of channels for lessons.

The number of courses can also be reduced by grouping related programs with a common core of beginning courses. This is easily accomplished in fields such as health, engineering technology, business, and secretarial training. Differentiation would then take place in the third and fourth semesters.

Despite the wide variety of alternatives to low-enrollment classes provided by the above methods, there is always the possibility that a student may need a low-demand class. An instructor may undertake to supervise the work of a student (especially a promising one) engaged in independent study; or a Learning Resources Center staff member may work out a study program; or the college may provide an examining procedure of its own or adopt one such as the College Level Examining Program (CLEP) whereby a student may demonstrate his competency for the purpose of receiving credit in a subject area. In many colleges all these situations are handled by the Learning Resources Center.

Small classes cannot always be eliminated. In nursing programs, state regulations often impose a limit of ten students to an instructor for the clinical classes conducted at a hospital. Equipment, space, and safety requirements also have a bearing on class size. Departments offering such programs may compensate for these small classes by increasing the size of others, for example, a beginning or orientation class in nursing, appreciation classes in music and art, and band, orchestra, and choral classes in music.

Colleges may also control the no-show student problem in restricted enrollment classes by imposing a nonrefundable fee that is applicable to a student's tuition and fees. Finally, placing responsibility on a department to maintain an overall average of weekly student contact hours keeps small classes under control, does not injure the program, and keeps costs in balance. This balancing of large and small classes also enables colleges to maintain a comprehensive program, although those that operate under collective-bargaining agreements with class size limits would have difficulty using this method.

Colleges or departments that use various autotutorial systems of learning and open laboratories do not have much difficulty with low-enrollment classes. However, some overbuilding of these facilities has taken place and their use in the afternoon hours is no greater than that in the regular classrooms.

The charge can be made that by controlling low-enrollment classes, financial considerations have become paramount, which leads to the elimination of courses that often have more relevance to the educational program than popular courses. The suggestions outlined above attempt to overcome these objectives. Opportunities exist for continuing such low-appeal but vital courses and programs, provided faculty and administrators are willing to make the accommodations required not only by today's financial difficulties, but by consideration of the reasonableness of the cost.

Chapter XV

❀❀❀❀❀❀❀❀❀❀❀❀❀❀❀❀❀❀❀❀❀❀❀❀❀❀

Moratorium on New Colleges and Buildings

Just as external phenomena were a major cause of the financial crisis, so too will they contribute to the end of the difficulty. The external phenomenon most likely to help ease the strain is the declining rate of population growth. Such a decline has already been reflected in a lower rate of enrollment growth and now, increasingly, in an absolute decline.

In the short run, operating unit costs may rise since internal adjustments lag a year or so behind, but in the long run costs will stabilize or go down. Capital-outlay expenditures should show a steep decline during the next five years.

Until the beginning of this decade the consequences of the long-term trend of the declining rate of population growth made little impression on most community college educators. Few expected a reversal of the yearly enrollment increases that resulted in the quadrupling of enrollment between 1959 and 1971. Hardly anyone paid attention to a report issued by the Arizona State Board of Directors for Junior Colleges. Based on eight years experience, the board announced that since its concern at the time was "saturation rather than insufficient provisions for the enrollments of the next decade, we believe that a moratorium of not less than five years should transpire after 1969 before additional junior college districts are established" (1969).

Until 1970, this view had few adherents among community college educators. Instead of a moratorium, they advocated creating more colleges, citing the constantly expanding enrollment statistics, the larger proportion of high school graduates going to college, the diversion of freshmen from senior institutions because of cutbacks and closings, and the untapped sources of potential students. In a series of reports, the Carnegie Commission on Higher Education also stressed the need for more community colleges. In 1970 it estimated that by 1980, 230–280 colleges should be established if the goal of a "community college within commuting distance of every potential student is to be achieved" (1970, p. 35). In a 1971 report, the range was adjusted to 175–235 (Carnegie Commission on Higher Education, 1971a, p. 5). In its 1970 report the commission did add: "Caution seems especially appropriate in view of the fact that entirely new types of educational experience beyond high school may develop in the future, attracting some of the students who might otherwise enroll in community colleges" (Carnegie Commission on Higher Education, 1970, p. 35). Unfortunately, this caution was ignored by the press and educators. In spite of reservations, the commission believed that other factors would counteract the effects of the demographic trends that point to a decrease in the eighteen-to-twenty-one-year age group by 1980. Consequently, their recommendations for expansion had a positiveness that few questioned.

The National Center for Educational Statistics predicted community college enrollment will increase from 1.63 million in the fall of 1970 to 3 million in the fall of 1980, almost an 85 percent increase (*Chronicle of Higher Education,* Apr. 17, 1972, p. 1). Ironically, the same issue of the *Chronicle of Higher Education* carried an article stating that "colleges will still have openings next month for at least 500,000 new freshmen, if recent trends hold true."

In the face of these pronouncements and predictions, a moratorium may seem unrealistic, if not foolhardy. For some states and communities this may be true; they will have to start new colleges if open access to higher education is to become a reality, as the Carnegie Commission points out. Nevertheless, if new colleges must be established, consideration should be given to the use of temporary buildings, perhaps on the order of 20 percent of the total square footage. This will conserve financial resources and make it possible to cut back on space on comparatively short notice should the need arise. Temporary buildings are also easier to sell and less expensive to raze. It is becoming increasingly evident that a moratorium on new buildings is more urgently needed than one on new colleges. Educators must improve the use of classroom space and help reduce the need for capital-outlay funds.

While a moratorium may prove unpopular in many states, it is becoming a distinct possibility. In the fall of 1970, the optimism of community college educators was shaken by disappointing enrollments. The hope that this was a minor deviation began to dissipate as the decline in the rate of increase, or absolute decline, continued and spread to more colleges in 1971 and 1972.

In March 1972, before a Joint Hearing of Representatives of Senate and House Appropriations Committees, President Gannon of Lansing Community College testified that "the State has nearly adequate physical plants and teaching facilities to meet the needs for liberal arts education in community colleges and four-year colleges and universities," and that "present enrollment studies indicate a downturn in enrollment in the late 1970s and early 1980s" (pp. 8, 9).

While educators were advocating the establishment of new colleges, a slowdown was in effect. From the peak year of 1968 when ninety-one new colleges were reported the number dropped to twenty-five in 1971. For 1972 the *AACJC Directory* listed only seven as scheduled to be opened. A comparison of the number of colleges operating in 1970 and 1971 showed that sixteen states had the same or fewer two-year institutions in 1971 as in 1970.

Considering the September 1971 and 1972 experiences of many colleges, the census reports, and the declining growth rate in the public schools, the call for a moratorium by the Arizona State Board of Directors for Junior Colleges may prove to be one of the most prophetic statements made by a community college group. It must have taken a good deal of courage to make such a public pronouncement, when nearly every educator and educational group was predicting unlimited expansion. Unless educators use restraint, more will be embarrassed by facilities that are grossly underutilized.

A moratorium on new colleges and buildings alone will not solve the financial crisis; but it will relieve the states and local communities of the heavy commitments they incurred during the peak years of growth. The 1973–1974 federal budget contains no appropriations for higher education facilities (*Chronicle of Higher Education,* Feb. 5, 1973, p. 1).

Chapter XVI

Increasing Faculty Productivity

Another class of economies affects the teaching and learning process, the area of education in which the greatest expenditures occur. These economies depend upon increasing the productivity of the faculty by increasing the number of students taught by an instructor or the number of class hours per week assigned; by changing the teaching-learning process so that student learning is partly or wholly independent of the instructor; or by a combination of these.

Increasing class size or applying management principles to

the teaching-learning process is not popular with faculty who maintain that the "profit/loss-debit/credit approach to education . . . presumes that students are little more than inanimate objects within a time and motion study" (*Read On,* 1972, p. 1). They are wary of projects that have cost-effectiveness as one of their purposes, viewing them as threatening and as evidence of attempts "to reduce operating expenses at the cost of quality education, if necessary." Thus, for example, only after the term "cost-effectiveness" was discontinued from a proposal did the faculty senates of the California Coast Community College District agree to participate in a project for facilities, utilization, and staff effectiveness (Brightman, 1971, p. 58).

Whether or not arguments against an increase in faculty productivity are based on economic or educational considerations, administrators face a formidable task in efforts to achieve their goal. On the economic issue, they must contend with strong faculty organizations, college senates, and affiliates of state and national organizations. Administrators also face the long tradition of education associating reasonable teaching workloads with high-quality student learning. The absence of criteria for measuring that quality has not diminished the fervor with which this belief is held, by many administrators and economists, as well as faculty.

Two major factors determine faculty productivity—the number of teaching hours per week and the average number of students per class, the product of which equals the weekly student contact hours (WSCH). This measure, has more influence on the cost of instruction than any other, including instructor salaries. Secondary factors that enter into a faculty member's workload include office hours, service on committees, and attendance at departmental and faculty meetings. These duties will have an impact on productivity if they enable the college to reduce (or not to increase) staff in such areas as counseling and student activities; however, it is doubtful that nonclassroom responsibilities have any significant effect in reducing operating costs.

Average WSCH vary from 350 to 600 or more in colleges operating under the conventional classroom pattern of instruction, though variations exist within and among colleges. Large colleges without collective-bargaining agreements may have average WSCH of 450–600, while colleges with agreements seldom have more than 400. Small colleges tend toward WSCH of 300–400. In general, English composition, clinical nursing, journalism, and some technical-vocational courses will have lower average WSCH than history, political science, physical education, and psychology courses.

When an effort is made to increase productivity, the most common method employed is to increase the size of the classes. Faculty have been less resistant to this than to an increase in their weekly hour load. When given a choice between the two, they rarely choose larger hourly load. In fact, progress in increasing WSCH often comes by trading one for the other. Usually this only means an average increase per instructor of from ten to twenty WSCH rather than the spectacular numbers achieved by using large classrooms.

One college administrator convinced his faculty to increase average WSCH for the academic year 1971 to 570, or fifteen more than the average for 1970. A fifteen-student increase may seem small, but when multiplied by 200, the number of instructors, it produces three thousand WSCH, which is equivalent to five-plus instructors (3000 WSCH ÷ 555). Assuming a $15,000 average yearly salary, the college gained a saving of more than $75,000.

Achieving and maintaining high WSCH depends on a delicate balance between enrollment and instructors. Too few students or too many instructors bring WSCH down. For example, average WSCH in a college for the fall semester was 560, but for spring 1971, when enrollment decreased, it went down to 534, a difference of twenty-six. With a faculty of one hundred, the loss to the college in WSCH was 2600 or the equivalent loads of more than four instructors (2600 ÷ 560).

A similar condition occurred at many colleges during the fall 1971 and 1972 semesters. Administrators who made faculty assignments on enrollment projections that failed to materialize were embarrassed by low WSCH, which meant a higher per student cost unless adjustments could be made during the spring semester. If the enrollment plateau, lower rate of increase, or even lower enrollment experiences of the fall 1971 and 1972 semesters should continue, most administrators desiring to control costs will have to resort to a teaching assignment policy that underestimates the number of instructors that will be needed. Otherwise, "very subtle changes in average load (as measured by student contact hours)' can have dramatic effects on the costs of operation" (Tadlock Associates, Inc., 1971, p. 11). Along with conservative hiring, administrators will have to select faculty capable of instructing in more than one discipline.

Another way of increasing average wsch is to eliminate marginal classes and programs. This was discussed in Chapter Fourteen. Increasing wsch by adding students to the normal classroom and eliminating marginal classes and programs is the method most commonly used by administrators to effect economies. It requires little in the way of extra equipment and no very large lecture halls—costly items that are beyond the means and needs of small colleges and that cut into savings when used by large colleges.

A method of increasing faculty productivity which advances well beyond the modest adjustments in wsch just described is to enlarge the classroom into a forum and modify the instructional pattern through various personnel and material aids. The forum type of classroom or auditorium is usually equipped with electronic devices enabling the instructor to regulate lighting; control screens; and communicate with the projectionist to display charts, film clips, or short reels. Other paraprofessionals may help him with bookkeeping chores such as recording attendance; preparing charts, tests, and other aids; grading papers; and the host of other activities ancillary to teaching. This method of increasing faculty productivity has greater possibilities in a large rather than in a small college. In a small or medium-size college capital costs and ancillary services may be too high to offset the savings in teaching costs. Also, to be effective, a large forum type of classroom should be utilized for approximately 75 percent of the time college is in session.

In this expanded classroom concept the lower unit cost of instruction flows from the practice of assigning a large number of students to an instructor for two of the three hours a class is scheduled, and a smaller number for discussion groups for an additional hour. For example, in a forum type of class of three hundred students the instructor generates 600 wsch (2 hours × 300). Adding a one-hour smaller section of thirty students brings the total to 630. The instructor is awarded six hours or double-time credit for this assignment. Under the conventional system, an instructor with two three-hour-per-week classes of thirty students generates 180 WSCH (6 hours × 30 students). Under this plan, the extra costs for technicians and other services provided for the forum-instructor must be deducted from the savings.

Berchin (1972) compared the instructional costs of large group courses and the more conventional modes in seven districts. Of fifteen courses surveyed in which a college offered the course under both modes, eleven showed a lower cost per student for the large group and four a higher cost. The median cost of the large group was $31.28 per student versus $40.68 for the conventional group. The higher cost of the four large group classes over the conventional classes calls attention to the fact that economy of size may be lost if costly equipment is required or if instructors are given excessive contact-hour credit or special stipends for reorganizing the conventional course for large lecture purposes. However, Berchin's evidence and the experiences at other colleges leave little doubt that large group classes tend to have lower per student cost than the conventional small group classes (p. 24).

Berchin also tried to determine the relative effectiveness of the two modes of instruction. Using as criteria student grades and percentage of students completing the course, he found that on both criteria the large group classes had the same slight, but not significant, edge, eight to seven, in higher student grades and in higher percentage of students completing the course. He concluded that "from the objective data . . . one can draw no conclusions about which institutional plan (large group or conventional classes) is more effective in learning outcomes" (p. 24).

The use of closed- and open-circuit television in teaching may be considered an extension of the large forum classroom. Through this medium thousands instead of hundreds of students may be enrolled in a class. Also, in a closed-circuit arrangement a course can be continuously offered in special rooms or may be available for viewing whenever desired by the student.

A large number of colleges use television in teaching but few have been able to achieve significant economies. A few colleges keep costs within reason whey they are able to get free time from a commercial station. Often they must accept early morning hours for broadcasting their courses. Even under these conditions production costs are high. To offset these high costs, a consortium of colleges may be formed to offer a few courses. One of the largest consortiums composed of twenty-two southern California colleges has been offering two courses a semester for five years using the facilities of a commercial and a nonprofit station. One course is telecast on four different time schedules; the other on two.

Some colleges are investing large sums in studios with highly paid directors and technicians. Usually, these colleges have or hope to get an educational broadcasting license.

The successful experience of TV College of the Chicago City College demonstrates the potential of television as an alternative to the campus classroom. Since 1956, TV College has enrolled 180,-000 individuals in eighty courses, including 80,000 for full college credit, and has awarded the A.A. to 350 students. Retention varies from 75 to 80 percent and performance is one-half grade better than that of adults of comparable ability taking conventional courses on campus (Zigerell, 1972). Among community colleges, TV College has maintained the most extensive instructional television program for the longest period of continuous operation. Its success educationally may account for the renewed interest in instructional television. In spite of all this, TV College has not materially reduced per capita cost. In 1969–1970 the cost per FTE at TV College was $1469, slightly higher than the Chicago District average of $1444 (Illinois Junior College Board, 1971d, p. 7). Colleges may use television for reasons other than reducing costs. Within limits a college may incur additional costs to provide courses to those unable to come to the campus, to extend its adult education and community service programs, to videotape lectures for the autotutorial learning centers and student performances in speech classes, and for other purposes.

From the evidence now available the general conclusion is that instructional television has not yet proved its potential for reducing educational costs nor does the evidence indicate its superiority over the conventional methods of instruction. Colleges find that cost and technical difficulties are their major problems.

The frequent criticisms for failing to increase productivity cannot be ignored. Educators and economists make a strong case for increased productivity as the key to the solution of the financial crisis. In a 1972 report the Carnegie Commission estimated that "raising the average [student-faculty] ratio by one would, by itself, reduce costs by about 0.3 percent per year per student—or nearly one-third of the total reduction we recommended of 1 percent per year" (1972, p. 17).

The economist, Schultz, argues that "the present conventional view that the educational sector is destined to continue as it is in the amount of time required of students and teachers may be as wrong," as a similar view of a few years ago concerning the productivity of farmers and retail employees (Schultz, 1971, pp. 19–20). Finally, Machlup points out that "if the technology of education remains unchanged—so that no more students can be taught per teacher—the cost of education per student must increase in perpetuity, and the rate of increase will vary directly with the rate of economic growth" a condition that cannot continue indefinitely (1970, p. 95).

Administrators and faculty have felt the impact of these efforts to improve faculty productivity; in fact, many administrators are less reluctant than formerly to discuss it. They are asking their faculties questions that point to the heart of the financial problem. Consequently, some faculty are becoming aware of the consequences of tight budgets and the resistance of taxpayers. They have a growing realization that the economy is having trouble supporting universal higher education on a ratio of twenty to thirty students per faculty member, and are heeding critics who are challenging the low hourly teaching load and student-faculty ratio. As a result, classes are increasing in size and very small classes are fewer in number; the movement to reduce class-hour loads has abated; and experimentation with autotutorial, paraprofessionals, systems development, television, and individual instruction is more common. But acknowledging this in no way changes the previous statement that the road ahead in this direction will be bumpy.

Predictions beyond the present decade on the success of increasing productivity are difficult to make—as well as hazardous. The examples cited prove that teaching loads can be increased. Other successes will follow as long as the increments are small and workload adjustments reasonable.

In states hampered by collective bargaining, changing the labor-intensive characteristic of education will encounter serious opposition. Little can be expected in this direction from the colleges situated in such states. Any breakthrough in the improvement of faculty productivity will have to come mainly from the larger number of colleges that are not yet covered by restrictive agreements.

The contention that increased productivity makes possible larger faculty salaries does not carry much weight. In private enterprise the direct relationship may exist, but not in education. In fact, an inverse relationship might be shown. Rewards for increased productivity have generally been in the form of fewer hours of teaching instead of a substantial increase in salary. Salary schedules, based on academic preparation with built-in automatic step increases, do not encourage differential rewards for productivity partly because administrators have not developed a system of merit rating, and partly because faculty organizations are opposed to differential salary schedules. It is also questionable whether taxpayers would countenance a system providing salaries commensurate with such productivity if the salaries were larger than the going rate in other colleges. No community college has taken seriously the Ruml-Morrison concept of large salaries for increased productivity in number of students taught (Ruml-Morrison, 1959, pp. 33–43).

Though compelling reasons exist for a change in teaching technology, increased faculty productivity will not be an immediate or easily implemented reform. The long tradition equating low teaching load with quality is not easily abandoned.

Chapter XVII

❀❀❀❀❀❀❀❀❀❀❀❀❀❀❀❀❀❀❀❀❀❀❀❀❀

Changing the Teaching
and Learning Process

The process of adding students to a class does not change the technology of teaching. To bring about dramatic increases in faculty productivity, the roles of the instructor and the student in the learning process are being changed. Although experimentation with a variety of new learning techniques has been going on for more than ten years, only one has ever attempted a complete substitution of a new learning model in place of the traditional teacher classroom practice; the others are doing so with modifications. In the experiments the objectives are twofold: to improve the learning of students and to reduce the cost of the learning process. The first used to be a paramount; during the last five years the second has become equally, if not more, important.

Basic to, and an integral part of, most of the plans is the development of behavioral objectives: the spelling out of goals, acceptable methods of measuring student achievement, and faculty accountability for student achievement. A second aspect of these new plans is the change in the role of instructor from one of continuous contact with students to one of managing a team of paraprofessionals and developing learning materials in small units that students may use at their convenience. To comply with state laws, students may still be officially enrolled in a course for three, four, or five hours per week over a definite period of time, but in practice they are free to come and go as they please provided they complete the units of work for the course.

An important change in California makes it possible to receive state aid for students enrolled in classes under a System, Instruction, Coordinated (sic) plan that combines "teaching methods, including the use of mechanical and electronic devices, self-instructional materials and/or other similar teaching techniques to convey a particular area of knowledge or skills from the instructor to the student . . ." (California Community College, 1972, p. 30). This means an instructor is not required, as formerly, to be physically present in the classroom.

The reduction of costs proceeding from this systems approach and from other plans discussed here depends on the use of lower-paid paraprofessionals in the learning laboratory under the supervision of an instructor who is available for consultation and other responsibilities.

Interest in the new technology of teaching is so widespread that directories or inventories of instructional programs and materials are being produced in various parts of the country. Experimentation with programmed self-instruction is no longer exceptional in colleges. While several colleges are producing materials for sale, equipment and packaged materials are also available from publishers and manufacturers. Tarrant County Junior College in Fort Worth has issued a Directory of Packaged Instructional Materials, alphabetically listing items in use in its district colleges under eighteen subject headings from Art and Basic Studies to Spanish and Speech. A nationwide inventory—*A Directory of Self-Instructional Materials Used in the Junior College* (1971)—was so popular that an enlarged, revised edition is now available. The directory lists twenty-three subject areas alphabetically, including technical-vocational, general education, and liberal arts programs and units. Some programs cover entire courses, others particular segments of courses (Sheldon and Park, 1972). At the same time, workshops on instructional systems, media, management, and evaluation are becoming common. A 1972 Carnegie Commission on Higher Education Report calls this development "The Fourth Revolution," succeeding the piece of chalk and the blackboard, lantern-slide projector, and tape recorder in the language laboratory (*Chronicle of Higher Education,* Feb. 7, 1972, p. 1).

Not all these new technologies and methods of teaching lead to increased productivity nor are all administrators willing to subordinate the instructor's role as much as is required to achieve large cost savings. Paraprofessionals in education are becoming as common as those in the medical and legal professions. They include tutors for remedial students; readers for English composition classes; technicians and aides in autotutorial laboratories in typing, shorthand, reading, biology, speech, and foreign language; laboratory assistants in the physical sciences; and various aides in the forum type of classes. So far though, in many colleges, tutors, readers, and laboratory assistants are additions to the staff; to help the instructor perform his duties more effectively but not to increase his productivity. This increases rather than decreases the cost of instruction. Where this occurs, administrators and faculty seem satisfied that the improved instruction resulting from the use of paraprofessionals warrants the extra cost.

A similar observation can be made about the new media or learning resources centers that are being established in most colleges as adjuncts or integral parts of the library. The media centers and laboratories are repositories of learning aids available to students and faculty on the same basis as the library. But just as libraries are seldom thought of as means for increasing faculty productivity, neither are media centers. Even for colleges that are concerned with increasing faculty productivity, the danger exists that after installation of elaborate equipment, it may remain idle for lack of trained personnel and failure of the college to develop programs adapted to the equipment. The situation would essentially repeat the same mistakes many made in the premature purchase or lease of data processing, television, and computer equipment.

The most widely heralded experiment in the systems approach to learning was initiated in September 1965 at Oakland Community College in Michigan (Tirrell, 1967). On an institution-wide basis, the founders of the college, aided by an independent consulting firm, applied the audiotutorial plan introduced at Purdue University by S. N. Postelthwait in his botany classes (Postelthwait, 1967). The emphasis was on self-instruction, with only a limited number of group sessions for orientation or discussion. Large areas with carrels replaced all but three traditional classrooms.

A comprehensive program of courses were offered with emphasis at the beginning on the liberal arts plus a few technical vocational programs, including registered nursing. The clinical aspects of the nursing program by necessity had to be conducted at nearby cooperating hospitals.

At the opening of school in September 1965, 4,000 students enrolled. All were involved in this new learning process; there was no other option. The founder believed that in a mixed system of the new with the old, the new method of learning would not survive.

To prevent bending the system he was convinced that "at least in the initial stages of development, a small group must exercise tight controls over the system (Tirrel, 1967, p. 61)." The organization was highly centralized with a president determined to prove that the systems plan could be applied to the entire college —ultimately to three colleges in the district—and two vice presidents.

The vice president for curriculum had total responsibility for designing and selecting the instructional system, which then had to be approved by and accepted for implementation by the vice president for campus administration. Thereafter, the campus administration vice president had total responsibility for system and student performance evaluation. Instructional materials were developed by a small group of faculty who were really part of the management group. At the learning level were the faculty members and tutors who helped the students. In the first year, 150 administrators and faculty members were involved in the introduction of the system.

The large areas which replaced the classrooms were equipped with carrels, audio-tapes, visual displays, books, periodicals, laboratory experimental set-ups, and programmed materials and manuals in small units for each subject taught. Students were self-paced, moving from one unit to the next after they passed a written or oral test administered by the instructor assigned to the area. The instructor was also available for consultation.

Students met in large group assemblies on a scheduled basis under a master teacher who discussed course objectives, presented new developments in the field, and pointed out applications of the subject matter. A major purpose of these assemblies was to motivate the students and create a feeling of group identity. Small class sessions were used mainly for testing and discussion. (I have relied heavily on Tirrell, 1966, 1967, for this description of the Oakland plan.)

Many factors may have contributed to the failure of the experiment. High priority among the causes was the lack of knowledge or model for implementing an industry format in an educational setting. Second to it was the highly centralized organization in which faculty played a minor role in policy formation or curriculum planning. For example, the first teaching packages were supplied by an outside firm; the later packages were written by the staff with the aid of the firm. Students did not prove as self-motivated as the system required. Absences, dropouts, and failures were high. Poor financial management, inadequate supervision of accounting personnel, and failure to maintain proper records were also alleged. The cost to the district of unused programs and carrels has been estimated at one million dollars (Lehto, 1972a, 1972b).

In spite of the costly failure of the plan, many of its features have been incorporated in programs throughout the country, especially in those involving auto-tutorial methods with extensive use of media, individual instruction, functional teaching teams of instructors, and paraprofessionals. In its early days the college was a mecca attracting large numbers of educators interested in the new technology of learning. Oakland College together with its predecessor, the Postelthwait audiotutorial laboratory at Purdue, probably have had the greatest influence in popularizing this new technology among community college educators.

For Oakland, however, the experiment ended in 1968 when the founding president resigned. Oakland Community College reestablished the traditional model of instruction with classes conducted by instructors. The old buildings were remodeled and new buildings designed to conform to the needs of the traditional model. Moreover, the district is operating under a collective bargaining agreement with a strong clause defining faculty workload in terms of maximum weekly classroom teaching hours, class size, and weekly student contact hours leaving little room for a return to the systems model initiated in 1965.

A few colleges are edging toward an Oakland type of college-wide systems approach. One that is making the attempt is South Oklahoma City Junior College which opened in September 1972. Instructors who are employed sign contracts that commit them to this method of instruction and require a production of 1200 weekly student contact hours (Cleek, 1972).

One learning laboratory that has gone even further than Oakland College in reducing the role of the instructor was recently organized at Orange Coast College in California. The college is taking advantage of a change that makes it possible to receive state aid for students enrolled in classes under a System, Instruction, Coordinated (SIC) plan that combines "teaching methods, including the use of mechanical and electronic devices, self-instructional materials and/or other similar teaching techniques to convey a particular area of knowledge or skills from the instructor to the student" (California Community Colleges, 1972, p. 30). What this means is that an instructor is not required, as formerly, to be physically present in the classroom. Basic arithmetic, elementary algebra and trigonometry combined, are scheduled for six hours a day. Students enroll in one of these courses on a "five hours arranged basis."

Two hundred and fifty students are assigned for five hours a week to the laboratory which is supervised by a paraprofessional for six hours a day, five days a week. Usually six different instructors are assigned to the laboratory with a maximum of three hours per week of instructor-assigned time allocated. They are available during their regular office hours for professional consultation during the time the lab is open. An instructor assigned to one of the six programmed courses is given one-half hour of assigned time from his weekly contact hour load to select programmed materials, modify procedures, review tests, review the success of programs and the like. At maximum capacity the laboratory generates 1250 WSCH. A comparison of salary costs for the laboratory with conventional classroom teachings methods is given in Table 6.

Berchin (1972) identified and compared the direct instructional costs between twenty matched courses under individualized programs and conventional modes of instruction, and also between fifteen matched courses under audiotutorial and conventional modes of instruction. In the first group of matched courses he found that costs were lower in fourteen of the individualized courses and in six of the conventional courses. The median cost per student for the programmed courses was $63.27; for the conventional, $74.63. In the second group the expenses were lower for nine of the audiotutorial courses and for six of the conventional courses, but total median cost per student was higher for the audiotutorial than for the conventional—$83.08–$81.31. In the same study, Berchin found the percentage of students completing the conventional courses was higher than for either the individualized program courses or the audiotutorial courses. Students in nine individualized courses received better grades than those in the conventional courses, while students in five conventional courses did better than those in the programmed courses. Students in the conventional courses outperformed those in the audiotutorial by the same ratio, nine to five (pp. 51, 83).

As with the Berchin study on relative cost of forum versus normal classes the results are inconclusive. Costs in audio tutorial clases can be higher than in the regular classes because of large start up costs, especially in equipment and professional and technical employees. Low enrollment will cause costs to rise in audio tutorial classes as in the regular classes. Also, a college administrator who is convinced that better learning results in audio tutorial classes may feel that within reason higher costs are justified. However, costs can be reduced if that is the purpose of introducing the audio tutorial

Table 6.

SALARY COST COMPARISON OF LABORATORY LEARNING
AND TRADITIONAL CLASSROOM METHODS

	Laboratory	Traditional
Learning Laboratory Method		
Salary of one paraprofessional for one semester (assuming a semester salary of $4500)	$4500	
Salary equivalent of instructor assigned time 1/5 of $7500 (assuming a fifteen-contact-hour teaching load and a semester salary of $7500)	$1500	
Total salary cost	$6000	
Traditional Classroom Method		
Cost for a semester for 1250 WSCH (assuming 500 WSCH load per instructor) equals 1250 WSCH ÷ 500 WSCH = 2.5 instructors × $7500		$18,750
Comparison of Salary Unit Cost per WSCH		
Conventional classroom $18750 ÷ 1250 WSCH =		$15.00
Learning laboratory $ 6000 ÷ 1250 WSCH =		$ 4.80

Source: Fitzgerald, 1972.

system of instruction. (See the previous discussion of Orange Coast College.)

The inconclusive results on quality confirm the experiences of other investigators who have studied the effectiveness of various methods of teaching (Dubin and Traveggia, 1968, p. 10).

Apart from the savings made available by experimental

laboratory courses, large savings can be achieved in the conventional science laboratory. By employing laboratory supervisors instead of instructors, the president of Muskegon Community College, Michigan, estimated that the laboratory cost per student semester could be reduced from $69.85 to $41.70 (Greene, 1971, p. 4).

Laboratory costs may be reduced in two other ways. The most common method is to eliminate or modify the requirement that all students in a science course enroll in a laboratory section. Non-science majors are allowed to enroll in the regular science courses without enrolling in the laboratory sections, or they may enroll in special science courses in which a few laboratory demonstrations are performed by the instructor. In either case, large savings are effected with the reduction of the number of laboratory sections that usually have low enrollments and are expensive to equip.

In the second, less widely utilized practice, science students are permitted to use the laboratory at any time of the day. A biological laboratory, for example, may be used by beginners and advanced students at the same time. Such open laboratories reduce the number of teaching stations by at least 50 percent; require less equipment; and minimize cost by efficient use of materials and staff. This practice forms an integral part of instructional methods under the autotutorial and other independent study plans (Hunter, 1971, p. 30).

Chapter XVIII

❀❀❀❀❀❀❀❀❀❀❀❀❀❀❀❀❀❀❀❀❀❀❀❀❀❀❀❀❀

Nontraditional and External Degree Plans

During the 1960s as the financial pinch became more painful, educators began exploring the advantages of utilizing off-campus, non-college-directed learning experiences. These innovative approaches to learning are in principle not new. Advanced placement, correspondence courses, credit by examination, independent study, credit for related work in business and industry or for military experience, instructional television, and computer-assisted instruction have been commonly subscribed to by the majority of educators.

Institutional plans widely used for granting credit are the College Proficiency Examination Program (CPEP) of the New York State Department of Education and the College Level Examination Program (CLEP) of the College Entrance Examining Board.

What these plans have in common is an emphasis on the assessment of what students know, rather than on the time they have spent in the classroom. For educators, legislators, and governors the appeal of the plans lies in the possible savings, especially in the area of instructor salaries and cost of facilities. Proponents claim that if these alternatives to traditional classroom education are used by enough students, the savings could rescue higher education from near bankruptcy. The widespread interest in nontraditional study being expressed by many states is a fairly reliable indicator that many educators are willing to give students the opportunity to use these alternatives.

At its December 1971 meeting, the Illinois Board of Higher Education approved staff recommendations that colleges "explore ways and means of integrating and crediting actual on-the-job and/or other life learning experiences, incorporating adult and continuing education programs within traditional curricular offerings" and that "equivalency testing be broadened and expanded" (Illinois Junior College Board, 1972b, p. 2). Since then, credit for on-the-job experiences has been broadened to include previous employment. In addition, the Junior College Board has adopted policies that enable colleges to grant up to thirty units of credit to students who achieve a test score on CLEP general examinations equal to the fortieth percentile, and a corresponding score of 460–470 as a minimum basis. Several colleges now follow this policy.

Aside from the widespread practice of granting credit for military experience, specific evidence is not available on the extent to which other nontraditional credit-granting practices are being utilized. However, their use has increased markedly. In 1971 more than twice as many students received credit from nontraditional courses as in 1970 (Peterson, 1972, p. 27). In Chicago alone 703 students earned a total of 7452 credits on one or more CLEP examinations during the 1971–1972 academic year. Since 1970, 14,676 credits have been earned through the examinations (*News of the City Colleges of Chicago,* 1972, p. 6). College-sponsored credit-by-examination plans are extensively offered to enrolled students who are permitted to challenge a course by taking an examination at any time for final credit.

A more extreme departure from the present method of dispensing learning and awarding degrees are the various forms of external degree, college-without-a-campus, and university-without-walls programs. More widely publicized than most are two New York plans which make it possible for a student to earn an associate or bachelor's degree solely by examination.

One of these is directly sponsored by the State University of New York (SUNY) and allows a student to earn his degree by independent study under faculty direction. The SUNY system functions through its experimental component, Empire State College, which has no campus in the traditional sense. Instead, the college, which awards both the associate and bachelor's degrees, has a headquarters in Saratoga Springs and four learning centers throughout the state near campuses, libraries, and laboratory facilities, with a total of twenty centers planned. The near-term projection is for an enrollment of 7000–10,000; for the long-term 40,000 is envisioned.

In some aspects, Empire State College is a system of learning centers within a system of colleges and universities. Each center has a dean, two assistant deans, thirteen faculty mentors, and "tutors who may or may not have traditional faculty qualification, but who are judged to have the most to offer the student." Since each center will admit only five hundred students, admission is on a first-come, first-served basis for high school graduates. Tuition is equal to that for resident students. Students have three options: all work off-campus; semester on-campus with off-campus study; off-campus study with seminars on-campus. Within each option students may choose one of three basic modes of learning: the discipline mode, the problem mode, or the experience mode (Carnegie Corporation of New York, 1971, pp. 19–23).

The second plan, the New York Regents External Degree, may be of greater import to community colleges since the first degrees, granted in 1972, were Associate in Arts based largely on credit by examination. Heavy reliance is placed on CPEP and CLEP. Students may earn credit for United States Armed Forces Institute courses, military service, knowledge or skills learned on the job, and artistic, literary, and musical accomplishments. Degree requirements include forty-eight units in the arts and sciences with a limit of twenty-seven in any one discipline, and twelve units of electives, which may include life experiences (Nolan, 1972).

Of the two plans, the Regents External Degree may be more difficult for the student, but it would effect the greater savings since it has a minimum staff and no college plants.

A third American plan in this category, the University-Without-Walls funded by the U.S. Office of Education, is a consortium of seventeen participating colleges, including Staten Island Community College. In this program, students may complete part of their work for a degree as an intern in a school, hospital, business firm, or the Peace Corps. They may also take courses in any of the participating colleges. Under a fourth plan, National Open University, regional confederations of junior colleges, colleges, and universities rely heavily on public broadcasting as the medium of instruction.

Interest in the external degree plans depends to a large extent on the hope that they will enable the states to reduce the outlays for education. This interest has been whetted by reports that the unit cost of instruction at England's Open University, Milton Keynes, is only one-fifth to one-fourth the cost at the average British university (Wagner, 1972, pp. 159–183; Maclure, 1971, p. 62).

The plethora of plans and proposals for alternatives to traditional education systems and study patterns inevitably led to a Commission on Nontraditional Study sponsored by the Educational Testing Service and the College Entrance Examining Board, supported by a grant of $140,000 over a two-year period from the Carnegie Corporation. The Commission's fifty-eight recommendations will serve as a guide for educators interested in nontraditional study (Commission on Non-Traditional Study, 1973).

From the wide range of options offered by the recommendations, educators of all persuasions can find one or more suited to their interests. Boldness is matched by caution; advocacy of new alternatives by support of traditional patterns. Thus in Recommendation 5: "The needs of some students for new options should not deny other students the option to stay within the traditional academic framework." The executive secretary of the Commission stated that the recommendations reflect the ambivalence between supporting "diversified opportunities" and a "desire to protect existing colleges and universities" (Jacobson, 1973). The report seems to be directed toward the interests and concern of the senior colleges rather than those of the community colleges, which is not surprising since the representation on the Commission was predominantly from those institutions.

The college-without-walls is a concept for the senior colleges and universities, although Associate in Arts degrees are given in the New York state plans and in other experimental plans such as the University-Without-Walls, the National Open University, and Chicago Television College. The current emphasis in the great majority of community colleges is for the most part offering credit for off-campus learning activity rather than a degree.

It is too early to make a prediction on the ultimate viability of these contemporary alternatives, but the prospects are not auspicious for the four-year colleges and universities. They are even less promising for the community colleges which, as open enrollment institutions, are already alternatives for large numbers of students. Serious criticism of the various plans is appearing more frequently than when the concepts were first proposed. The elaborate procedures and safeguards associated with some of them are likely to stultify initiative and increase costs of operations to such an extent that little financial benefits will accrue to the colleges. Implementation of plans has not been easy.

If one were to judge the impact of on-campus and off-campus nontraditional study experiments by past experience, one would not be optimistic about the future of present plans. So far instructional television, credit for nonclassroom learning, and correspondence schools have not proved serious alternatives to conventional classroom work, nor have they resulted in large financial savings for community colleges. Very often plans that appear in catalogs or in professional journals are not implemented because of faculty apathy or opposition, absence of student interest, administrative indifference or lack of commitment, or failure to set up the machinery required.

For many years community colleges have used an advanced

placement system in such courses as typing, shorthand, mathematics, and foreign languages, but until recently credit was rarely given for the elementary course (or courses) in the sequence. Even today, in many colleges, students who may be permitted to take an advanced course in a sequence are not given credit for a prerequisite if they have not learned it in a college classroom.

Moreover, most educators are making only minor changes in the learning process—modifying rather than drastically revamping it. A great deal of rhetoric is being written about changes, but essentially the bulk of the learning process takes place in the usual classroom setting with an instructor and a limited number of students. Where changes are taking place they often become supplementary aids to the traditional classroom learning process, thereby increasing costs rather than reducing them. To be effective in reducing costs, nontraditional study plans must become integral, rather than supplementary, to the learning process.

Nontraditional study, except on a minor scale, will become one of the many educational fashions that arouse enthusiastic interest for a time and then disappear with little effect on traditional education. Yet the possibility of a turnabout cannot be overlooked, since credit by other than classroom learning and the external degree plan has two advantages going in its favor—advantages that were previously lacking. One is prestige, resulting from sponsorship and promotion by the legislatures, state educational agencies, and foundations; the other is the urgent need for relief from the heavy financial outlays for education. This urgency may parallel experience of colleges after World War II, when veterans were granted credit for military experience and work done in military schools. The need then was to redress as much as possible the educational and economic losses suffered by veterans while serving their country. Granting credit for military activities was, and continues to be, an educational policy few colleges would venture to oppose.

Faculty reaction to external degree plans may only be conjectured since these plans seem to pose no immediately serious threat to community college instructors. In fact, outside New York State, external degree plans are still in the talking stage. Most of the criticism that has been raised so far has come from the senior colleges and universities, which voice great concern over the deterioration of academic standards. Those institutions are also afraid that legislatures will be tempted to consider the external degree only in terms of the possible savings offered in operating expenditures and capital outlays. Some educators are even questioning the claim that flexible space-time programs are less expensive than the normal programs (Bailey, 1972).

Epilogue

During the financial crisis community college educators have managed to balance their budgets and new colleges have been formed. Some have resorted to deficit financing, more would have done so were they not prohibited by state law.

In the analysis of sources of revenue, the point was made that educators cannot look to a substantial increase in state and local appropriations as a way out of the financial crisis. For the rest of the 1970s the prospects will at best be a repetition of the experience of the previous decade. Taxes are reaching a point of diminishing return. Demands on public funds for health, welfare, sanitation,

123

and other activities are just as insistent as for education. Inflation nullifies much of whatever increases in yearly appropriations the colleges receive.

Except for vocational-technical grants and student aid in its various forms, federal aid for operating expenditures seems more uncertain in 1973 than at any time since the 1950s. It may improve but not to the extent educators believe necessary to make a large contribution to operating income.

Tuition and fees to cover the cost of instruction offer an unattractive solution for an open-access institution committed to a policy of universal higher education. However, the charges keep getting higher and no-tuition colleges are becoming extinct. Provisions for remission of tuition and federal and state opportunity grants, work-study programs, and loans are making tuition more acceptable to community college educators. Though some advocate tuition to cover the cost of instruction, this possibility may come after the principle has been adopted by senior institutions. The transition from the present moderate tuition policy to full tuition will be not much more difficult than the transition from no tuition to the present policy (Richardson, 1972, pp. 25–26).

Private donations are a welcome source of revenues, but for the next few years they will not be of sufficient size or reliability to help in the solution of the financial situation.

Aside from minor changes, financial support patterns for community colleges will continue as in the past. Any proposed reform, short of massive federal aid and/or tuition charges equal to the cost of instruction, will not solve the financial crisis. Although the move toward full state support continues, transferring the cost from local districts to the state will merely shift the problem, not resolve it. State budgets are as strained as city and county budgets. The pleas of governors and mayors for federal aid are as urgent as those of educators. Colleges supported by the state are no better off than those whose revenues depend on the local property tax. Full state financing relieves property owners of the burden of supporting education, but others must assume it through taxes on income, consumer products, or luxury items; through lotteries, on- and off-track betting and other forms of gambling. The advantage of this diffusion of income sources is that it may make it more difficult for these new taxpayers to combine against education than it is for the property owners to do so. On the other hand, state legislatures and governors may be less subject to pressure for increased appropriations.

The proposal for a statewide property tax would equalize the tax burden and help provide minimal basic education for most persons by eliminating the discrepancies between the amounts available in the various districts.

Since educators are not able and cannot expect to receive sufficient funds, they have had to turn to cost-cutting strategies.

The most direct method of balancing the budget is the traditional pattern to curtail programs, reduce staff, and make no significant upward adjustment in salaries. The teaching and learning process remains unchanged. Most administrators concentrate on reducing expenditures through improved administrators and accounting procedures, reduction in building, closer attention to utilization of facilities, and modifications of the teaching-learning process. Of these the last is undergoing the greatest scrutiny because it absorbs almost 75 percent of the budget.

The many options available to educators range from adding students to an instructor's workload without changing the traditional teacher-student classroom relationship, to a learning system which subordinates the role of the instructor and places greater responsibility on the student. Whichever of these options is chosen, common to all of them is a reduction in instructors. Some educators believe that the resolution of the financial problem will come not from changes that add a few students to the instructor's workload but from a basic transformation of the learning process through a systems development model along the lines attempted on a college-wide scale at Oakland (Michigan) Community College. This type of model represents the kind of change Machlup was thinking about when he wrote that by the year 2000 he would "not be surprised to find that capital has been substituted for labor in the area of education as it has in other sectors of a growing economy. The faster the economy grows, the faster rises the cost of education and the faster will these methods be replaced by others that economize human resources" (1970, p. 100). If this should happen, an educational revolution without historical parallel will have occurred.

For the foreseeable future most of the economies in the

teaching-learning process will be in the less spectacular and less revolutionary methods that involve an increase in the instructor's workload. Even this is encountering resistance from the faculty as collective bargaining spreads.

The rise of strong faculty organizations and the legalization of collective bargaining, mandatory in some states, are serious hindrances to economy moves touching the teaching workloads or the role of instructors. It will be suprising if educators are able to substitute capital for labor in their enterprise during this century. Negotiated collective-bargaining agreements do not warrant optimism for Machlup's prediction.

Collective bargaining also restricts college administrators in other respects. When contracts are negotiated statewide as in Hawaii or districtwide as in Chicago, campus administrators have only minimal opportunity to influence their terms. Second, contracts change the administrator-faculty relationship forcing on administrators shared responsibility. Before the advent of collective bargaining, shared responsibility was dependent on the beneficence of administrators. Moreover, as collective bargaining spreads, nearly every area of administration or decision making becomes a subject of bargaining.

Reports of prolonged strikes makes educators not under contracts anxious to avert collective bargaining. They are trying to stave it off by enlarging the decision-making role of faculty and by matching or exceeding the salaries and fringe benefits in colleges covered by contracts. This is a difference in form rather than substance. The quite undesirable effect on the financial situation is very much the same.

The reports of prolonged strikes also indicate that administrators are not acceding to demands as readily as in the early years of collective bargaining and that they may be making demands of their own. In the Allegheny County Community College strike of 1972 the administration threatened to shut down operations for the semester. As administrators gain experience with collective bargaining, they will more frequently counter demands for salary increases with demands for increased productivity. What may be happening is the development of an effective form of shared responsibility in which issues are resolved on the basis of merit rather than on the strength of one or the other party in the negotiations. More experience with negotiations is necessary before a truly effective shared-responsibility process develops.

Financial relief may depend upon phenomena not subject to control. An effective solution may emerge from a value change that higher education is not the highest good for all people. If adopted widely, the suggestion that young people delay entrance to college for a year or more will help relieve the financial crisis. Many of those who delay will never enter college, thus reducing the number and cost; the one year delay will have a temporary effect on cost and a permanent effect if those who do return are as well prepared in attitude, aptitude, and experience to do college work. A rationale is being developed that dropping out between high school and college is a healthy condition for the student as well as for society (*Phi Delta Kappan,* 1971; Babbot, 1971).

Some critics are attacking the institution itself, claiming that education does more harm than good. Abetting this movement are those who question Americans' preoccupation with higher education, arguing that some of the money spent on higher education might be better utilized for purposes such as clean air and water, transportation, health care, and social services (Alden, 1971). More broadly, Schultz asserts that "propositions about [the benefits of] education that have long been treated as self-evident and settled are placed in doubt" (1971, p. 15). Then there is the disenchantment of many young people who find education irrelevant.

The declining enrollment in senior colleges and universities is creating more competition among admission officers in recruiting high school graduates. Not only are some institutions lowering admission standards but they are also offering financial aid and work-study grants as inducements to enrollment as freshmen. How effective this is in diverting students from community colleges is not known.

Also pertinent is the competition that may come from the proprietary schools, many of which are now controlled by well-financed corporations such as Bell and Howell, Xerox, and CBS. Little is known about the number of schools or their enrollment. But, the concern has surfaced as a result of the 1972 federal legislation making students of proprietary schools eligible for federal grants (*Chronicle of Higher Education,* May 14, 1973, p. 3). The immediate concern of community college educators is the competition for federal funds; in the long run the diversion of students may be of greater concern.

There is the more likely possibility that a static or declining population will result in a slowing down in the rate of enrollment increase and in the rate of expansion of colleges. Some states are reaching saturation in percentage of high school graduates attending college, a demographic phenomenon that may prove to be one of the most effective solutions to the financial crisis.

What combination of causes will bring about a resolution of the financial crisis can only be conjectured. The causes of the crisis in any situation bring about corresponding adjustments. The probability that marginal institutions may be forced to close is one of the possibilities in this adjustment. Colleges in overbuilt multi-campus districts as well as colleges in declining rural areas may be the victims.

Much of this discussion is conjectural depending to a large extent on trends, projections, political climate, economic situation, attitudes on marriage, child-bearing, family size, and many other factors. That these may change, sometimes dramatically, makes forecasting hazardous. Today's trends, projections, attitudes, mores will probably not persist any longer than yesterday's.

References

Academic Senate for California Community Colleges. *Legislative News-letter.* 2:3, January 25, 1972.

ALDEN, V. R. "How Much Is a College Education Worth?" *The Wall Street Journal,* Sept. 1, 1971, p. 8.

American Association of Community and Junior Colleges. *1973 Community and Junior College Directory.* Washington, D.C., 1973.

Arizona State Board of Directors for Junior Colleges. *We Believe: Arizona and Its Community Junior Colleges.* Phoenix, Ariz., 1969.

Arkansas Commission on Coordination of Higher Educational Finance. *A Study of the Need and Recommendations for the Development of a Comprehensive Community College in Pulaski County,*

Arkansas. Little Rock: The State Community Junior College
Board, 1970.

ARNEY, L. H. *State Patterns of Financial Support for Community Colleges.* Gainesville, Fla.: Institute of Higher Education, University of Florida, 1970.

BABBOT, E. F. "Postponing College: Alternatives for an Interim Year."
College Board Review, Summer 1971, pp. 21–29.

BAILEY, S. K. "Flexible Time-Space Programs: A Plea for Caution." In
D. W. Vermilye (ed.), *The Expanded Campus: Current Issues
in Higher Education 1972.* San Francisco, Jossey-Bass, 1972.

BERCHIN, A. *Toward Increased Efficiency in Community Junior College Courses.* Los Angeles: League for Innovation in the Community College, 1972.

BOGARD, L. "Management in Institutions of Higher Education." In A.
Mood (Ed.), *Papers on Efficiency in the Management of
Higher Education.* Berkeley: Carnegie Commission on Higher
Education, 1972.

BOWEN, W. G. *Guidelines for 1971–1972 Budget Requests.* New York:
Management Division, Academy for Educational Development,
1970.

BRIGHTMAN, R. W. *Strategies for Change: Case Studies of Innovative
Practices at the Coast Community College District.* Costa Mesa,
Calif.: Office of Educational Development, Orange Coast College, 1971.

BROWN, D. G. "Finding New Dollars in Old Budgets." *The Chronicle of
Higher Education,* May 15, 1972, *6,* 8.

Cabrillo College. *Morning and Evening Class Schedule,* Aptos, Ca.,
Spring 1972.

CALAIS, M. J. *Possible Positive Results of the Current Financial Crisis
in Higher Education.* Speech given at the American Association
of Higher Education's 27th National Conference, Chicago,
Mar. 1972.

California Bureau of Junior College Administration and Finance.
"Junior College Income Sources: Fiscal Year 1964–65, 1965–
66, 1966–67, 1970–71." Sacramento: Division of Higher Education, 1971.

California Community Colleges. *Handbook of Definitions: California
Community Colleges.* Sacramento: Office of the Chancellor,
1972.

California Junior College Association. *CJCA News.* Feb., 1971, *16,* 1.

Carnegie Commission on Higher Education. *The Open Door Colleges:*

Policies for Community Colleges. New York: McGraw-Hill, 1970.

Carnegie Commission on Higher Education. *New Students and New Places: Policies for the Future Growth and Development of American Higher Education.* New York: McGraw-Hill, 1971a.

Carnegie Commission on Higher Education. "New Roads to a College Degree." *Annual Report.* New York: 1971b.

Carnegie Commission on Higher Education. *The More Effective Use of Resources: An Imperative for Higher Education.* New York: McGraw-Hill, 1972.

Carnegie Corporation of New York. *Annual Report 1971.* New York, 1971.

CHADWIN, M. L. *The Illinois Public Junior College System: Program Review January 1973.* Springfield: Illinois Economic and Fiscal Commission, 1973.

Change. Jan./Feb. 1971, *3,* 13–14.

CHAPMAN, C. E. *Some Observations: Presentation to Fall Faculty Conference, 1971.* Multilithed. Cleveland, Ohio: Cuyahoga Community College, 1971.

CLEEK, J. *A Common Sense Approach to Education: A Comprehensive Plan for the Development of South Oklahoma City Junior College.* Oklahoma City: South Oklahoma City Junior College, 1972.

Coast Community College District. *A Comparison of Selected Financial Statistics of California Community College Districts, 1968–69.* Costa Mesa, Calif. 1969.

Coast Community College District. *A Comparison of Selected Financial Statistics of California Community College Districts, 1970–1971.* Costa Mesa, Calif., 1971.

Coast Community College District. "Selected Financial Statistics of California Community College Districts, 1971–1972." Costa Mesa, California, 1972.

COHEN, A. M. *Dateline '79: Heretical Concepts for the Community College.* Beverly Hills, Calif.: Glencoe, 1969.

Commission on Non-Traditional Study. *Diversity by Design.* San Francisco: Jossey-Bass, 1973.

Committee for Economic Development. The Research and Policy Committee. "A Statement on National Policy." *Saturday Review,* Jan. 14, 1967. *50,* 38.

COOMBS, P. H. *The World Educational Crisis: A Systems Analysis.* New York: Oxford University Press, 1968.

CROWL, J. A. "Court Ruling on Property Tax Could Affect Community College Financing." *Chronicle of Higher Education,* October 26, 1971, p. 1.

Current (Florida Association of Community Colleges Newsletter). May 1972, *4,* 2–3.

Cuyahoga Community College. *Financial Statements.* Cleveland, Ohio, June 30, 1971.

DEEGAN, W. L. Memorandum to California Junior College Association Board of Directors, Superintendents and Presidents of Member Institutions. Sacramento, Sept. 28, 1971.

Developing Junior Colleges. Mar. 26, 1971, no. 88, 1.

DUBIN, R., AND TAVEGGIA, T. C. *The Learning Teaching Paradox: A Comparative Analysis of College Teaching Methods.* Eugene, Ore.: Center for Advanced Study of Educational Administration, 1968.

DWYER, W. G. Personal communication. June 27, 1972.

Education Commission of the States. *Bulletin,* June 1973, *6,* 2.

Educational Facilities Laboratories. *Bricks and Mortarboard: A Report on College Planning and Building.* New York, 1964.

Financing Virginia's Colleges: Current Operating Income and Expenditures 1970–71. Richmond: State Council of Higher Education, 1972.

FITZGERALD, J. Personal communication. April 24, 1972.

Florida Department of Education. *Ten Years of Selected Data for Florida's Public Community Colleges.* Tallahassee, Fla.: Division of Community Colleges, 1971.

GANNON, P. J. *Excerpts of testimony before Appropriations Committee.* Lansing, Mich.: Lansing Community College, 1972.

Genesee Community College. *Memo.* June 21, 1972.

GLENNY, L. A. "The Anonymous Leaders of Higher Education." *Journal of Higher Education,* Jan. 1972, *47,* 16.

GOLD, B. K. *Survey of California Community College Evening Enrollments.* Research Study 72–9. Los Angeles: Los Angeles City College, 1972.

GREENE, C. M. *A Forward Thrust: The State of the College—An Opportunity for the Future.* A report by the President of Muskegon Community College. Muskegon, Mich., 1971.

HAMILL, R. E. Personal communication. Oct. 9, 1972.

Harrisburg Area Community College. *President's Progress Report.* Harrisburg, Pa., 1970.

HARTFORD, E. F. "The State of the Community College System (1964–

1970)." In C. W. Burnett (Ed.), *The Two-Year Institution in American Higher Education.* Lexington: College of Education, University of Kentucky, 1971.

Hawaii University. *Controlled Growth for the University of Hawaii Community Colleges. Policy Statements by the Board of Regents of the University of Hawaii.* Honolulu, 1970.

HEFFERLIN, JB L. "Reform and Resistance." Research Report 7, Washington, D.C.: American Association for Higher Education, 1971.

Higher Education in the States. Oct. 1971, *3*, 58.

Higher Education in the States. Apr. 1972, *3*, 59.

HILL, D. W. *Proposed Formulas and Allocations of Funds, 1972–73 Budget.* Xeroxed copies. Chicago: Chicago City Colleges, 1972.

HUNTER, W. *Budgeting for Educational Development: A Ten-Year Report of Experience from St. Louis.* St. Louis, Mo.: Junior College District of St. Louis, 1971.

HUTHER, J. W. "The Open Door: How Open Is It?" *Junior College Journal,* Apr. 1971, *41*, 24–27.

Illinois Junior College Board. *Operating Financial Data of the Illinois Public Junior Colleges for 1971–72.* Springfield, Ill.: Office of Research and Management Information Systems, 1971a.

Illinois Junior College Board. *College Bulletin.* Jan. 1971b, *5*, 3.

Illinois Junior College Board. *College Bulletin.* Feb. 1971c, *5*, 4.

Illinois Junior College Board. *College Bulletin.* Aug. 1971d, *6*, 7.

Illinois Junior College Board. *College Bulletin.* Dec. 1971e, *6*, 3.

Illinois Junior College Board. *Report of Selected Data and Characteristics of Illinois Public Junior Colleges 1970–71.* Springfield, 1971f.

Illinois Junior College Board. *Annual Report 1971.* Springfield, Apr. 1972.

Illinois Junior College Board. *College Bulletin.* Jan. 1972b, *6*, 2.

Illinois Junior College Board. *College Bulletin.* Sept. 1972c, *7*, 5.

JACOBSON, R. L. "Colleges Are Not Meeting Needs of Adults, Panel on Non-Traditional Study Finds." *Chronicle of Higher Education.* February 5, 1973, p. 7.

JENSEN, A. M. *Budget Preparation, 1970–71.* Mimeographed. Memorandum to Division Chairmen and Administrators. San Bernardino, Ca.: San Bernardino Valley College, Dec. 1969.

JENSEN, A. M. *Budget Preparation, 1971–72.* Mimeographed. Memorandum to Division Chairmen and Administrators. San Bernardino, Ca.: San Bernardino Valley College, Jan. 1971.

JENSEN, A. M. *Budget Preparation, 1972–73.* Mimeographed. Memorandum to Division Chairmen and Administrators. San Bernardino Ca.: San Bernardino Valley College, Jan. 1972a.

JENSEN, A. M. Personal communication. Mar. 28, 1972b.

JOHNSON, B. L. *Islands of Innovation Expanding.* Beverly Hills, Ca.: Glencoe, 1969.

KIBBEE, R. J. "Answering the Tuition Advocates." *The City College Bulletin.* Apr. 1973, *68,* 11–13.

KOLTAI, L. *The Impact of National Defense Education Act, Title III on the Instruction of Foreign Languages in California Public Junior Colleges.* Los Angeles: University of California, 1967.

Legislative Newsletter. Jan. 1972, *2.*

LEHTO, N. J. "OCC Finance Report: $64 million = 2,200 Grads." *The Daily Tribune* (Royal Oak, Mich.), June 6, 1972a, pp. 1, 3.

LEHTO, N. J. "OCC Programmed Learning: Educational Mess!" *The Daily Tribune* (Royal Oak, Mich.), June 7, 1972b, pp. 1, 2.

LEHTO, N. J. "OCC Classrooms Empty Half the Time." *The Daily Tribune* (Royal Oak, Mich.), June 8, 1972c.

LOMBARDI, J. *The Financial Crisis in the Community College.* Topical Paper No. 29. Los Angeles: ERIC Clearinghouse for Junior Colleges, 1972.

LOMBARDI, J., AND TRIGG, C. W. "Classroom Utilization on an Overcrowded Campus." *Junior College Journal,* Feb. 1951, *21,* 338.

Los Angeles Times. Jan. 31, 1970, part II, 6.

Los Angeles Times. Jan. 31, 1971a, Sec. A., 29.

Los Angeles Times. Oct. 21, 1971b, part II, 7.

Los Angeles Times. Mar. 22, 1973, part I, 1.

MC DANIEL, J. W. "Sidewalk College." In B. L. Johnson (Ed.), *The Experimental Junior College.* UCLA Junior College Leadership Program, Occasional Report No. 12. Los Angeles: University of California, 1968.

MACHLUP, F. *Education and Economic Growth.* Lincoln, Neb.: University of Nebraska Press, 1970.

MC HUGH, W. F., AND O'SULLIVAN, R. *New York Community College Collective Negotiation Contract Survey.* Albany, N. Y.: State University of New York, 1971.

MACLURE, S. "England's Open University: Revolution at Milton Keynes." *Change,* Mar./Apr. 1971, *3,* 62.

MC PHERRAN, A. L. *Junior College Income Sources: Fiscal Years 1965–66, 1966–67, 1967–1968.* Sacramento: California Bureau of Junior College Administration and Finance, Division of Higher Education, 1969.

MARTIN, A. H., AND THORNBLAD, C. E. (Eds.) *Report of Selected Data and Characteristics of Illinois Public Junior Colleges, 1969–70.* Springfield, Ill.: Junior College Board, 1970.

MARTIN, M. Y., Director, Community College Education, Office of Education. Interview, Feb. 24, 1973.

MESSERSMITH, L. E. "CJCA Position Statement on Legislation." Memo to all concerned. Feb. 14, 1972.

Michigan, State of. 76th Legislature. Regular Session of 1971. Enrolled Senate Bill No. 105. 1971.

Michigan Community College Association. *Community College Enrollments, 1971–1972.* Research Series vol. 72, no. 1. Lansing, Mich., 1971.

MOYNIHAN, D. P. "The Impact on Manpower Development and Employment of Youth." In E. J. McGrath (Ed.), *Universal Higher Education.* New York: McGraw-Hill, 1966.

Nation's Business. "How the States Are Attacking the Welfare Mess," July 1971, *39,* 58.

New York, State University of. *Geographic Origins of Students, Fall 1969.* Report No. 12. Albany, New York: Office of Institutional Research, 1971.

New York Times Apr. 14, 1973.

News of the City Colleges of Chicago. May/June 1972, *5*:6

Newsweek. Mar. 22, 1971a, *78,* 63.

Newsweek. June 7, 1971b, *78,* 102.

Newsweek. July 30, 1973, *82,* 50–58.

NOLAN, D. J. "University of the State of New York: Regents External Degrees." *Compact,* Oct. 1972, *6,* 3–5.

Oakland Community College. *The Challenge of Change: Annual Report, 1969–70.* Bloomfield Hills, Mich., 1970.

Office of Research and Managerial Information Systems. *The Now Colleges in Illinois.* Springfield: Illinois Junior College Board, 1972.

Office of Research, Management Information Systems and Legislation. *Operating Financial Data of the Illinois Public Junior Colleges for 1971–72.* Springfield, Illinois: Illinois Junior College Board, 1972.

O'NEILL, J. *Resource Use in Higher Education: Trends in Output and Inputs 1930 to 1967.* Berkeley: Carnegie Commission on Higher Education, 1971.

Oregon Board of Education. *Business and Support Services, School and College Finance and Statistics.* Salem, Ore., 1971.

Oregon Community College Association. *Oregon Community Colleges Policy Makers Guide, 1971–1972.* Part 1. Salem, Ore., 1972.

ORWIG, M. D. (Ed.) *Financing Higher Education: Alternatives for the Federal Government.* Iowa City, Iowa: American College Testing Program, 1971.

PETERSON, R. E. *American College and University Enrollment Trends in 1971.* Berkeley: Carnegie Commission on Higher Education, 1972.

Phi Delta Kappan. Sept. 1969, *53*:50.

POSTELTHWAIT, S. N. "An Audio-Tutorial Approach to Teaching Botany." In B. L. Johnson (Ed.), *System Approaches to Curriculum and Instruction in the Open Door Colleges.* UCLA Junior College Leadership Program, Occasional Report No. 9. Los Angeles: University of California, 1967.

QUIE, A. *Address to the Seminar on Postsecondary Occupational Education; Federal Programs for the 1970s.* Arlington, Va.: American Vocational Association and the American Association of Junior Colleges, 1970.

Read On. Apr. 18, 1972, *1*, 1–2.

RICHARDSON, RICHARD C., JR. "A Reaction to the Commission Recommendation." in D. V. Vermilye (ed.), *The Expanded Campus: Current Issues in Higher Education.* San Francisco: Jossey-Bass, 1972.

RICHARDSON, R. C., JR., BLOCKER, C. E., AND BENDER, L. W. *Governance for the Two-Year College.* Englewood Cliffs, N.J.: Prentice-Hall, 1972.

ROLLINS, C. E. "Fiscal Planning at the Community College Level." Speech delivered at the Seventh Annual Conference of the Society for College and University Planning, Atlanta, Aug. 1972.

RUML, B. R., AND MORRISON, D. H. *Memo to a College Trustee.* New York: McGraw-Hill, 1959.

RUSSELL, J. D., AND DOI, J. I. *Manual for Studies of Space Utilization in Colleges and Universities.* Athens, Ohio: American Association of Registrars and Admissions Officers, 1957.

School Management. July 1968, *12*, 34.

SCHULTZ, T. W. "Resources for Higher Education: An Economist's View." In M. D. Orwig (Ed.), *Financing Higher Education: Alternatives for the Federal Government.* Iowa City, Iowa: American College Testing Program, 1971.

SHANNON, J. "School Finance Reform: ACIR View." *Education Commission of the States Bulletin,* November 1970, *3*, 1–2.

SHELDON, M. S., AND PARK, Y. (Eds.) *A Directory of Self-Instructional Materials Used in Community Colleges.* (2nd ed., revised) Los Angeles: University of California Danforth Junior College Program and ERIC Clearinghouse for Junior Colleges, 1972.

SHOEMAKER, E. A. "Community Colleges: The Challenge of Proprietary Schools." *Change,* Summer 1973, *5,* 71–72.

SIMON, K. A., AND GRANT, W. V. *Digest of Educational Statistics 1971 Edition.* Washington, D.C.: Department of Health, Education and Welfare, 1972, pp. 100, 104.

SPENCER, T. *Sources of Income for Community College Capital Outlay 1970–1971.* Little Rock: Department of Higher Education, 1972a.

SPENCER, T. *Sources of Income for Community College Current Operation 1970–1971.* Little Rock: Department of Higher Education, 1972b.

State University of New York. *Rules and Regulations Governing the Administration and Operation of Community Colleges.* Albany, 1972.

STEINER, P. O. "At the Brink: Report on the Economic Status of the Profession." *AAUP Bulletin,* June, 1971, *57,* 241–242.

Tadlock Associates, Inc. *Organizing for Tomorrow: A Management Study for Triton College.* Los Altos, Calif., 1971.

Texas, State of. *Education: Texas' Resource for Tomorrow.* Report of the Governor's Committee on Education Beyond the High School. Austin, 1964.

Texas Research League. *Financing a Statewide Community College System in Texas.* Austin, Texas, 1970.

TICKTON, S. G. "Managing Higher Education Better." *Education Technology,* May 1971, *11,* 13.

TIRRELL, J. E. "(Total!!) Independent Study at Oakland." *Junior College Journal,* Apr. 1966, *36,* 21–23.

TIRRELL, J. E. "Some Reflections on 150 Man-Years Using the Systems Approach in an Open-Door College." In B. L. Johnson (ed.), *Systems Approaches to Curriculum and Instruction in the Open-Door College.* Los Angeles: University of California Graduate School of Education, 1967.

TOOMBS, W. *Productivity and the Academy: The Current Condition.* University Park: Center for the Study of Higher Education, Pennsylvania State University, Apr. 1972.

U. S. News and World Report. Oct. 20, 1969, *67,* 36.

U. S. News and World Report. Jan. 31, 1972, *72,* p. 60–78.

Vermont Regional Community College Commission, Inc. *Annual Report.* Montpelier, Vt., 1972.

WAGNER, L. "The Economics of the Open University." *Higher Education,* May 1972, *1,* 159–183.

WATTENBARGER, J. L., CAGE, B. N., AND ARNEY, L. H. *The Community Junior College: Target Population, Program Costs, and Cost Differential.* A National Educational Finance Project. Gainesville, Fla.: Institute of Higher Education, University of Florida, 1970.

WITMER, D. R. "Cost Studies in Higher Education." *Review of Educational Research,* 1972, *42,* 107–108.

YOUNGER, F. L. Personal communication. May 10, 1972.

ZIGERELL, J. J. "The Television in Education." *The Community Services Catalyst,* Spring 1972, *2,* 33–40.

Index

A

Accountability and public attitudes, 2-3

Accrediting associations, expenses related to, 12, 13

Administration: business managers in organization of, 75; expenses related to, 11-12

Administrators: criticisms of, 12; reduction of, 68-70

Advisory Commission on Intergovernmental Relations, 33

Alabama, tax increase failure in, 2

Alaska, state support in, 26

ALDEN, V. R., 127

Allegheny County Community College, strike at, 126

American Association of Community and Junior Colleges, 36

American Association of Junior Colleges, 6, 11

Arizona, state support in, 21, 24

Arizona State Board of Directors for Junior Colleges, 96, 98

Arkansas: federal funds in, 18; tax increase failure in, 2

ARNEY, L. H., 25

Auxiliary services: control of costs in, 68; as revenue source, 56

B

BABBOTT, E. F., 127

BAILEY, S. K., 122

139